The Spiritual Path to True Success

The Practical Mystic's Guide to Living Successfully

Henry Thomas Hamblin

Hamblin Vision Publishing

Copyright

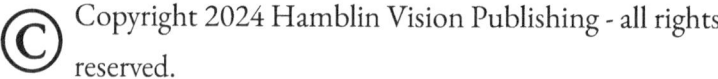 Copyright 2024 Hamblin Vision Publishing - all rights reserved.

The content contained within this book may not be reproduced, duplicated or transmitted without direct written permission from the author or the publisher.

Under no circumstances will any blame or legal responsibility be held against the publisher, or author, for any damages, reparation, or monetary loss due to the information contained within this book, either directly or indirectly.

Legal Notice:

This book is copyright protected. It is only for personal use. You cannot amend, distribute, sell, use, quote or paraphrase any part, or the content within this book, without the consent of the author or publisher.

Disclaimer Notice:

Please note the information contained within this document is for educational and entertainment purposes only. All effort has been executed to present accurate, up to date, reliable, complete information. No warranties of any kind are declared or implied. Readers acknowledge that the author is not engaged in the rendering of legal, financial, medical or professional advice. The content within this book has been derived from various sources. Please consult a licensed professional before attempting any techniques outlined in this book.

By reading this document, the reader agrees that under no circumstances is the author responsible for any losses, direct or indirect, that are incurred as a result of the use of the information contained within this document, including, but not limited to, errors, omissions, or inaccuracies.

Contents

Introduction	VII
By Noel Raine, Chair of the Hamblin Trust	
Concise Biography of Henry Thomas Hamblin	IX
By John Delafield, Hamblin's grandson	
Preface	XXII
by Henry Thomas Hamblin	

Part 1: The Fundamentals of True Success

1. Overcome and Conquer Now	2
2. Aspire	7
3. The Mental and Spiritual Causes of Success	15
4. Vision and Mental Imagery	26
5. Use Your Imagination	33
6. Overcoming Circumstances	36
7. Opportunity	44
8. Success Through Service	52
9. Work and Action	58
10. Equity, Justice and the Law of the Square Deal	65
11. Character Building	70

12. The Value of Optimism and Cheerfulness	75
13. Making Use of Infinite Power	81

Part 2: Healing the Hard Times Consciousness

14. Spiritual and Metaphysical Aspects	84
Spiritual and Metaphysical Aspects	
15. Psychological and Practical	93
16. The One Power of Infinite Good	105
17. Laying Up Treasure	113
18. Right Versus Wrong Methods	125
19. Laws Which Must Be Obeyed	132
20. Practical Instructions	136

Part 3: True and Lasting Success
From Simple Talks on Science of Thought No. 8

21. True and Lasting Success	147
22. Also by Henry Thomas Hamblin	154

Introduction

By Noel Raine, Chair of the Hamblin Trust

H T Hamblin was a prolific author of a range of books, booklets and pamphlets offering practical advice on how to live in harmony with God, or what he sometimes referred to as *Source, the Universe,* or *the Cosmic*. However, this was not just a spiritual quest, or an attempt to avoid the troubles and cares of everyday life – far from it, for Hamblin was a very practical mystic – but a practical guide to each one to follow to increase health, happiness, and prosperity.

Hamblin founded the *Science of Thought Institute,* offering a course of practical lessons intended to guide his many thousands of students towards a happier, healthier and more prosperous life and, although he is sadly no longer with us in person, he left a wonderful legacy of publications that he had written from 1921 up to the time of his death in 1958. Some of those are still in print and available from **The Hamblin Trust** on **www.thehamblinvision.org.uk** but many have since gone out of print.

Conscious that the Trust will not be around forever, the custodians of Hamblin's teachings, the trustees of the Hamblin Trust, have decided to produce copies of Hamblin's earlier works in digital format to leave a legacy for future generations. Whilst the style of writing may now seem a little dated, Hamblin's teachings remain valid and, although edited a little to bring them more into line with current editorial style, we are pleased to bring to you in one compilation, three of Hamblin's original booklets offering a guide to success in life:

- The Fundamentals of True Success (First published in 1923)

- Healing the Hard Times Consciousness (First published in 1931)

- True and Lasting Success [*Simple Talks on Science of Thought no. 8*] (1928)

It is our hope that this compilation will, indeed, help **you** to achieve success in **your** life.

Many blessings for health, success and happiness.

Noel Raine

Chair of the trustees
The Hamblin Trust

Concise Biography of Henry Thomas Hamblin

BY JOHN DELAFIELD, HAMBLIN'S GRANDSON

Who was Henry Thomas Hamblin?

Henry Thomas Hamblin was a spiritual teacher and writer based in Sussex, England, whose message and vision were straightforward and pragmatic. He believed that the spiritual life and the practical, everyday life were inseparable. His teachings centred around the power of thought and the importance of meditation to draw on the inner power, wisdom and love that we all have deep within us. Hamblin referred to this as "the Secret Place of the Most High" in the days before meditation was widely practiced in the West.

Hamblin was colloquially known as HTH, and later 'The Saint of Sussex'. Whilst his teachings leaned towards esoteric Christianity, his philosophy was truly universal, embracing the truths of all faiths. The emphasis of his message is on finding the power of spirituality within us all, in the context of our everyday lives, rather than religion. As a young man, he reacted against the dogma of his strict, religious upbringing, and believed that religion often divided people, while spirituality united people. His teachings came from a place of pure empathy and compassion for humankind.

Henry Thomas Hamblin worked right up to the end of his life in 1958 and left a legacy that continues to this day, its voice as much needed now as it ever was.

A Wayward Child

Henry Thomas Hamblin was born in 1873 in Walworth, South East London, of Kentish parents, and was the second of two sons. His father was very religious, and his grandfather a minister of the Baptist Church. His mother, although of diminutive size, was reportedly "great of soul" and ruled the family with benevolent autocracy. The family was poor, very poor, like all those living around them in that district of London in the late Victorian era, and, despite their hard work, the only education that could be afforded for Henry was an elementary one. He followed this with a course in technology, which proved to be of inestimable value to a youth who was considered by his parents and teachers to be wayward.

"Unstable as water; thou shall not excel," his mother reproached him regularly. No doubt she intended it to shame her son into a regime of self-improvement, in keeping with child-rearing practices of the time, but it was hardly confidence-inspiring! "Slacker!" was the repeated insult from his elder brother. Wiser, more objective, heads might have paused for long enough to recognise a certain potential in the young boy who, at the age of nine, could attempt the writing of a school newspaper. He had also established himself as something of an elocutionist. Writing and speaking would both prove valuable skills in later life.

His adolescent years gave little indication of an error in the family verdict. "Henry the wayward" moved from one poorly paid post to another, idled in between dead-end jobs, succumbed to bouts of ill-health, and, before he had reached the age of eighteen, had displayed more than the usual "adolescent failings", according to his autobiography, *The Story of My Life*. From a modern perspective, all these Victorian euphemisms point to Hamblin being something of a "bad lad", an impression added to by his own heavy hints that he had been no stranger to drinking and carousing. He suffered terribly from pangs of regret following his periods of over-indulgence, so that "Henry the sinner" became "Henry the saint" – until the next time. His pronounced rebellious streak landed him in hot water more than once. He constantly pushed against the boundaries of the fire-and-brimstone brand of Christianity in which he had been raised, which he felt to be unbearably restrictive. Reading about his struggles with authority as a young man somehow makes the rather aloof spiritual writer he became more accessible and endearing; it's hard not to warm to someone who so openly confesses their own faults and shortcomings, especially in the tightly buttoned-up era in which he lived. He was inspired by books, many of which fired his worldly ambition and prompted his spiritual imagination.

What his parents and educators overlooked was that Hamblin was a young man with huge aspiration, flushed with a youthful zest for life, and inspired by a worthy ambition to rise above the rut of his circumstances. Although he pushed against his father's dogmatic and punitive style of practising religion, at heart, he was deeply religious. A person's early environment, education, and adolescent behaviour can often determine the course of their life. Youthful indulgences of one sort or another are inevitable. Hamblin's studies of the New Testament, which revealed that selfishness and hypocrisy, rather than indulgence, received greater condemnation by Jesus, would have been very much in his consciousness.

A Successful Businessman

There is no doubt that Hamblin had an enquiring mind, and this, coupled with a desire for scientific accuracy, enabled him to achieve success in his later endeavours in business. In this, despite his lack of education, he was bolstered by boundless faith and courage, which, coupled with a shrewd business sense, ensured that he succeeded beyond all expectation. In 1898, having taught himself opthalmics at night, he qualified as an optician and set up his first successful business as an optician, Theodore Hamblin (now Dolland and Aitchison), frequented by royalty, the rich and the famous.

Hamblin was a natural entrepreneur and a born risk-taker. By this time, he was also a family man. He married Eva Elizabeth in 1902, and they went on to have two sons and a daughter.

He enjoyed acquiring several businesses, all with insufficient capital, and relying on credit and goodwill. He took more pleasure in the thrill of the challenge than in the promise of monetary gain. Far from being downcast in the face of numerous setbacks, he thrived on negotiating obstacles which appeared insurmountable. As soon as the business was established and running smoothly, however, rather than being satisfied with financial security and the ability to provide for his family, Hamblin's interest started to wane. He felt a loss of the initial drive and motivation, his physical and mental health began to decline... until the next big idea came along and away he would charge again, all fired up and raring to go.

Throughout all his wild days of youth and high-risk business ventures, Hamblin felt a great tug towards discovering a deeper meaning to life, beyond that of the daily struggle to make ends meet. Propelled by his discontent, he became a driven seeker after truth. In his quest, he met other prominent thinkers of the time and formed lasting friendships.

As his business success grew, so did a gnawing sense of depression. It was as if there was something inside him that had not yet found a voice. Around this time, he discovered the New Thought movement and began to read their publications. Hamblin realised then that none of his worldly success had made him happy. He felt that a move from London to the coast would be beneficial. Shortly afterwards came the outbreak of the First World War, and Hamblin went off to serve his country, leaving his business in the care of others, almost with a sense of gleeful relief, strange though it sounds.

But it was the sudden and unexpected death of his younger son at the age of ten, in 1918, that brought him to rock bottom and to question everything.

A Very Practical Mystic

Hamblin was not a genius, and millions of other people have made good in the world with even less promising assets. But it was in the second half of his life, when Hamblin turned away from creating highly successful business enterprises to focus instead on the spiritual realm, that his unique combination of the pragmatic and the profoundly spiritual shone forth. He has sometimes been described as a very practical mystic.

Hamblin began writing in the 1920s. The words seemed to flow from him. He found that writing clarified his thoughts. One of his first books written in this new phase of his career was *Within You Is The Power*, which was to sell over 200,000 copies. Other books soon followed. Hamblin believed that there is a source of abundance which, when contacted, could change a person's entire life. As long as people blamed their external circumstances for any misfortune, they were stuck in the 'victim role'; but if they moved in harmony with their inner source, their life could be full of abundance and harmony.

Soon after this, Hamblin set up a magazine called *The Science of Thought Review*, based on the principles of Applied Right Thinking. He wasn't discouraged by the fact that he had no experience of editing or publishing. His experience had taught him that if the mind worked in harmony with the Divine, then everything you needed flowed towards you. Anyone with any business sense at all knew that to set up a magazine with a first print run of 10,000 copies would be a risky thing to do. But Hamblin was not risk averse, to put it mildly! He wanted to put what he believed into practice. The only magazine of its kind in the 1920s, it soon gained a worldwide readership. Among his friends and contemporaries that were to contribute to the magazine were Joel Goldsmith, Henry Victor Morgan, Graham Ikin, Clare Cameron and Derek Neville, all of them prolific and successful writers. Apart from his international subscribers, Hamblin had close ties to comparative spiritual thinkers in many other countries, especially in the U.S.

Although he had been brought up in a strictly religious family, he hadn't found any of the answers he sought in the Church. He realised that, rather than following any creed or dogma, which didn't work for him anyway, he had to look within himself. He found contact with 'Presence' and realised it held the key to the peace he was seeking. All the time, his search was leading him nearer to discovering the way his thoughts affected his performance and outlook.

During the General Strike of 1926, the Great Depression of 1929-32, and again in years after the end of the Second World War, many homeless, unemployed wayfarers came to the Hamblin household seeking relief and shelter. Henry and Elizabeth provided them with a simple meal, new boots and clothing, and money for the road. Known colloquially as 'The Saint of Sussex", Hamblin was a man who applied his spiritual principles to his everyday life. Practical Mysticism was Hamblin's life's work. He helped people in deeply practical ways to become less fearful, happier, and more successful in their lives. To this end, he wrote books like *The Antidote to Worry*. However, later in life he realised that whilst these books genuinely helped people, they were largely concerned with the personality. He then wished to go a step further and become more fully a truly 'practical mystic', so he wrote a spiritual course of 26 lessons, each with a definite theme presented in a systematic way. This was designed to move beyond the constraints of personality so that the soul could breathe the pure air of Spirit. What was needed, he felt, was 'a total surrender of ourselves to the Divine.' The course is available as the book *The Way of the Practical Mystic.*

The Power of Thought

Hamblin was at the forefront of the New Thought movement which was gaining pace in the early 20th century. He discovered that 'new thought' was, in fact, ancient wisdom, based upon the truth that has always existed since before time began. All great souls give voice to that timeless truth in a myriad of different ways. Hamblin urges us to "Think in harmony with the Universal Mind." In other words, he underlines the fact that truth is and cannot be changed depending upon our mood or our whim.

Hamblin realised that we need not only a positive frame of mind but an applied way of thinking - Right Thinking, as he termed it. What did he mean by that? Well, he wrote a book on it, *The Little Book of Right Thinking*, which is in its 17th reprint. Essentially, he defines Right Thinking as:

- Thinking from the Divine standpoint.

- Controlling the thoughts so they do not go off on negative tangents away from the Divine Truth, which is always positive.

- Replacing negative thoughts with positive thoughts

- Living in the consciousness that all is well; and as an adjunct to this, remembering that perfection exists as a reality now, and to think in the consciousness of that knowledge.

- Meditation or prayer is the highest form of Right Thinking.

- Ultimately, however, the aim is to get beyond thought, 'to enter ultimate Truth'.

He says, 'When we cease thinking, we glide out on the ocean of God's Peace. Thought brings us to the foot of the mountain after which we have to proceed by intuition'.

> *'Health, Wealth and Happiness. Isn't this something we all want, either for ourselves or for those dear to us? And yet, how many of us are struggling*

> *to reach or hold such a goal for a sustained period of time?'*

Hamblin's teachings explain how we can achieve all of these things, not by hard work and striving but by a simple change of thought. *Within You is the Power* is one of his simple but profound statements, and the title of one of his books.

Hamblin was a prolific author and had many thousands of followers studying and benefiting from his teachings and courses until his death in 1958. The simple principles contained in those teachings are as relevant today as they were when he was alive, and can still help us to achieve health, prosperity and happiness if we apply them conscientiously.

He died in 1958 in Chichester Hospital. The Hamblin Trust exists to this day to propagate the legacy of his work.

The Relevance of his Teachings Today

Hamblin was, essentially, a Christian mystic, yet his ideas about the simplicity and clarity of presence seem incredibly contemporary. He believed that the source of all wisdom is within us and all around us, and that this is the fundamental reality; there is no separation, and we are all one. His message and advice to all who read his work is that it is for everyone and is in harmony with the aspiration of all good people throughout time. Hamblin believed that there can be no finite creed of an infinite faith. Moreover, he suggests that, when creeds appear, true faith can be constrained.

He cautioned that if you seek God in prayer, the corollary is that you must have faith in Him. He often stressed that no prayer goes unanswered, and, although you may not get the answer requested, your prayer will be answered in some form. God is around us and within us, and this is the fundamental reality. He made it clear that, although human organisations come and go, God's laws are eternal, and that God is the quintessence of love, wisdom, and harmony. He expresses the clear view that "Blessed are they who believe and yet have not seen". The knowledge that God is born within us is fundamental to our understanding, and only by the loss of self can God be found. At the point a person surrenders his or her 'self' to God, it is then that a re-birth takes place and one's real life in God begins.

Some may question this view and ask: "What is this but the core teachings of the many brands of Christianity?" In response, Hamblin's view was that modern Christianity is a heterogeneous compound of the teachings of Jesus interwoven with historic pagan-based doubts and fears, litanies, supplications and more, all of which are closely guarded by a priestly hierarchy. These were strong views, and Hamblin does not disparage those who found them uncomfortable, as he says that churches are necessary and helpful for those who are succoured by them. Hamblin had a lifelong rebellious streak where authority was concerned, and this included the strictures of the Church. Hamblin would sometimes say that the Truth of the message of Jesus was so often wrapped up in dogma and creed that its purity and simplicity were obscured.

In his teaching, he states that first comes purity of intention, reminding his readers that one cannot serve God and Mammon. Either you trust God completely or you hedge your bets by having worldly alliances and a healthy bank balance. He maintains that trying to achieve both will impair spiritual development. Secondly, an individual's dedication to following God's path will require great patience, perseverance, faith and courage; but in following this path, the individual will develop forbearance and good will. He adds that other life experiences will follow naturally and lead to a developing compassion, which will enable the individual to radiate the love of God.

Where should we place Hamblin in the long line of mystics, seekers and finders? Perhaps it is rather impertinent to pose the question some 65 years after his death, but it is surely relevant to consider this point as, by any measure, he was an extraordinary person.

Remember that he was born into a life of poverty and obscurity but, despite a very limited education, by superhuman efforts of his imagination, he rose to wealth and secured an esteemed position in life, while all the time being aware of another "self" within him, a spiritual self. Dramatically, in the middle part of his life, he surrendered his material successes to follow his wider calling as a disciple of God. In this later life, he did not subscribe to any specific creed or form of religion. He was no haloed saint in the traditional sense, but he would have said, "What I have done, or rather what has been done through me, can be done by any person in the world according to their gifts and personal faith".

The essence of this teaching is that the latent power of God lies within everyone.

John Delafied is the grandson of Henry Thomas Hamblin and a retired RAF pilot. The majority of his childhood was spent living with his grandparents, Henry Thomas and Elizabeth Eva Hamblin.

Preface

BY HENRY THOMAS HAMBLIN

If I could only make others understand how easy it is to succeed!

Success forever waits to crown our efforts, and it does so, without stint and with overflowing measure, as soon as we fulfil certain conditions. What these conditions are is explained in this little book.

Success has not to be wrung from life by force and agonising struggle, but that is something that comes to us naturally as water flows from the mountains to the sea.

Abundant good is always seeking us, and when we remove the barriers, it quickly makes itself manifest. Rich and abundant success will assuredly crown every life when it is allowed to do so.

Learn then, O reader, the secret of true success.

H.T.H.

Part 1: The Fundamentals of True Success

Hamblin Vision Publishing

CHAPTER ONE

Overcome and Conquer Now

True success, like enjoyment, brings no regrets: like true happiness it is lasting: being based upon equity, justice and service, it does harm to no one, but rather brings benefits and blessings into other lives.

I believe wholeheartedly in successful action. If a person is in business, then let them not rest satisfied until that business is well grounded in success. If a person is a public speaker, then, for the sake of others, if not for his own, let them be as able and successful a public speaker as it is possible for them to be. If a person desires to be a philanthropist and altruist, then let them see to it that they are a good philanthropist, and as successful in their altruistic aims as it is possible to be. "Whatsoever thy hand findeth to do, do it with thy might", said a very great man long ago: in other words, be successful in the true sense of the word.

It is necessary for every man and woman to be successful. One who is not successful is a hindrance and a burden to his friends, a source of constant irritation to his relations. Is there anything more pitiable than a failure, either man or woman? What a sad thing it is to see a parent who cannot bring up their children properly. What a misery is the person who is a failure at his "job", or, having failed in business, has not the pluck to try again.

Men and women, we must be successful: we must push, overcome, build up, laugh at difficulty, rise from our failures, and live a life of purpose and true achievement. We cannot afford to be failures: we dare not let things slide, we must be up and doing, we must overcome and conquer, and the time to begin is NOW.

Consider what happens to the one who fails miserably in the battle of life. Instead of striving and struggling, and thus becoming strong and stalwart, he lets things slide; he chooses the easy path of least resistance. He drifts and flops through life, becoming a mere plaything of fate and circumstances. His willpower gets less: his moral fibre weakens: his inefficiency increases: his health declines. He shirks responsibility: he cannot face trouble: he finds it impossible to make decisions. Is there anything more pitiable in all God's beautiful universe than a failure?

Listen to his tale of woe! He is the most unfortunate of men. His brother was sent to a better school, was a favourite of the "governor", and now look at him rolling in money, while he - the failure - is kept by his friends. Pity me, he cries, see in me the victim of an unkind fate. I was born under an unlucky star: circumstances have been against me, the current of life has been too strong for me: fate has become my master. It is not my fault: other people failed me: things went wrong at critical times: ill luck has dogged my footsteps.

So, we leave him, still explaining why, although it is not his fault, his life has been a failure. He thinks, poor fellow, that the cause is in circumstances: he cannot see that the cause is within himself.

He may have been born under an unfavourable star: he may have had what the Theosophists call an evil Karma: he may even have had the disadvantage of unfavourable birth and parentage, but these need not have doomed him to failure. The worst failure the world has ever seen could have made a success of his life, if he had only realised that within him is a power that is greater far than any difficulty, which would, if it had been called upon, believed in and made use of, have revolutionised his life.

Men and women all, there is no difficulty in life too great for us to overcome. The Infinite One has arranged life so perfectly that no trouble or difficulty is of such magnitude that we cannot overcome it by using the power that is within each one of us. Difficulties and drawbacks are only to test our mettle, and all who believe they can succeed, and will trust in the power within them, will succeed, and there is nothing on earth that can stop their progress.

I wish that I could make many of my readers understand the greatness of the power within them. There is no greater power in a successful man or woman, than in an unsuccessful one; the difference is that the former makes use of it and believes in it, while the latter does not. Did you ever meet a successful woman who did *not* believe whole-heartedly in her inner self and the power within her? Did you ever meet a failure who did believe in his inner self and the power within him? Never, for such a thing is impossible.

The difference between successful people and unsuccessful is one of mind, of mental outlook, of belief, of faith, of vision, of principle, of character. Success does not depend upon circumstances, for if it did then all who were born into good or easy circumstances would be successful; yet the reverse is frequently the case, for poor boys mount the ladder of success, and the well-born slide down to the mud at the bottom. Success does not depend upon education, for if this was so the educated would always succeed and the uneducated fail: yet it is not so, as we all know.

Working people educate themselves in their spare time and rise to the highest positions in the land, while educated men, with university degrees, sell bootlaces and matches in our streets. Neither does success depend upon brilliant intellect, for the men of highest intellectual attainments are often passed in the race of life by those less brilliantly endowed. Success comes to everyone who realises that a power that is unlimited is within him, and that therefore, in the long run, he can never fail.

Men and women, we can all succeed. We each have this power within us. It is unlimited, inexhaustible, and can never fail us. It is greater than any difficulty: stronger than any opposition: all that is needed is faith in its potency and a willingness to trust it and make use of it. No longer need we be inefficient or our lives lacking in true success, for within us we possess a something which will, if we trust it, make us victorious over ourselves, our weaknesses and our circumstances.

Efficiency and success are divine qualities. Look through nature and tell me, do you find God a failure? Can you imagine God as a failure?

"Be ye perfect even as your Heavenly Father is perfect". Thus spake the Great One. Can a failure be described as perfect?

Chapter Two

Aspire

It is necessary for every one of us to aspire. To ever strive after higher and more perfect expression is a law of Nature: it is *the* law of evolution. Within each species lies hidden the perfection of the divine idea, and each bird, animal and plant is ever seeking to express this innate perfection more fully. What is true of a flower, a plant or an animal or bird, is true also of man. There is a divine urge within him which bids him aspire to higher and better things - to a fuller, richer, deeper and more spacious life. People can harmonise with the divine purpose of their lives only as they strive to rise. So long as they aspire, all the divine forces hasten to their assistance. The law of life is progress, unceasing, unending. To try to evade this law, either knowingly or in ignorance, is the way of disaster, mental, moral and physical.

Men and women all, no matter what our circumstances may be, we must aspire - we must be successful - we must forever strive after a richer and fuller life. Too many of those around us are treading the path of death, instead of fullness of life. They are not building character: they are not improving their minds: they are not developing their talents: they are not reading anything worthwhile; they're not assuming responsibilities. Instead, they are seeking the easy way of life: shirking responsibilities, avoiding difficult tasks, reading trashy literature, wasting their days in amusements that are innocent, yet really not worthwhile. Instead of aspiring, they are wasting the precious years. Since this time last year, they have not advanced an inch in knowledge, skill, wisdom or accomplishment. Could they but realise the truth, they would know that they have actually slipped back. "No progression is retrogression", the head of a successful business said to me, when I was a young man with a small and struggling business, which I was conducting without capital by means of a series of weekly miracles. I thought at the time that he was hard, but later I realised how true his words were. If a business is not growing, then there is something very seriously wrong with it, and the cause of its unhealthiness must be discovered and remedied. It is the same with each individual life: no progression is retrogression. We must either go forward or we shall slip back. If we go forward, we live a fuller life: if we hang back, we atrophy and disintegrate.

Progress has to be made in some direction. There are some who frown on material success, and who say that all efforts should be directed towards spiritual attainment. These have my respect. There are those who say that intellectual attainment is the great be-all and end-all of existence. These, too, I respect, because all progress is admirable. There are also those who make the pursuit of wealth or social ambition their only aim that. These, also, I respect, although I feel sorry that their efforts are not more wisely directed. Lastly, there are those who make no progress at all. They never strive, either to improve their mind, body, soul or circumstances. They drift hither and thither on the mysterious sea of life: mere flotsam and jetsam, useless, lifeless. Such have not my respect - only my pity.

Which class do you belong to, oh reader mine? Belong to any class but the last. All lives of endeavour lead upwards, but the life of placid acceptance, of no effort, leads downward to disintegration and death.

He is wise who makes progress in all directions: who achieves a well-balanced success by advancing spiritually, intellectually, and in the service of his fellows through the medium of business or profession or public life. To make progress in one direction only, is to dwarf and distort the life as a whole. A man who is spiritual and neglects his business is not dealing fairly by his wife and children. Therefore, whilst he pursues spiritual ideals, he is committing a moral wrong by failing to support those dependent upon him. A similar charge might be brought against one who pursues intellectual pursuits to the detriment of other departments of life. Such get estranged from their fellows, and also lose spirituality. A worse charge can be brought against the one who makes the pursuit of wealth the "be-all and end-all" of life, for he makes life difficult, through excessive wealth, for his dependants: he shrivels up his own soul and shuts himself off from culture and spiritual advancement. Yet in spite of these grave deficiencies, a person who develops a lopsided success is a far better character than one who drifts: who makes no effort to climb and achieve.

Progress of some kind MUST be made. Would that I could write these words in letters of fire across the sky. As I look around me and see the crowds who are drifting through life: frittering away their precious hours: throwing away their glorious opportunities, I long to shout in their ears: "Awake, thou that sleepest!" I long to tell them that life is not for mere passing pleasure but is a glorious and precious opportunity to build up character, through experience, and for striving after higher and better things. Make progress in *some* direction - any direction rather than none at all. Do anything rather than nothing at all. Make any sort of progress rather than drift and slip back.

The great point is this: that striving after success in any department of life builds character. While it is wise to build an all-round, well-balanced success, it is absolutely necessary that we aspire and strive after something that is at present above us. It is more important that we make progress than is the precise character of that progress. We must climb, we must advance, we cannot stand still. Would that I could get this into the hearts and minds and imaginations of the ordinary people! Would that I could arouse them from their bovine placidity! If only they could be awakened from their dreamy slumber and made to strive and conquer, they would cease to live at this poor dying rate: they would enter into a fuller, deeper, higher and richer life of overcoming and progress.

It is often urged that the mundane things of life are not worth striving for. Ambitions, when realised, are disappointing. Wealth, fame, these things satisfy not, and, in addition, bring care and often suffering. After all, 'tis said, to rise in one's profession, while it may satisfy one's vanity, does not bring happiness. A working man smoking a pipe, reading his paper before the kitchen fire, is often happier than a much sought-after professional man who moves in high society. True, but the point is this: those who aspire and succeed, build up character. One who rises in life, or who overcomes difficulties, or becomes more efficient: who conquers disadvantages of birth or station, is far stronger in character than one who does none of these things. No one knows, but those who have passed through it, what difficulties, trials and tests are met with along the path of success. No sooner is one difficulty overcome than another appears. To embark in business on little or no capital: to risk one's little all on a single idea, demands courage, faith, self-assurance: such a life makes a call upon all one's hope, persistence, perseverance and steadfastness. Time after time all may seem lost: time and again the situation is saved as by a miracle. The battle ebbs and flows, the issue hanging in the balance, until at last character and enthusiasm, faith, hope and persistence win the day, and the first stage of success is reached. Such experiences as these build up character. One who overcomes difficulties such as these, becomes strong and resourceful, and develops faith and vision. If, however, having won comparative success, a person rests on their oars, their character will deteriorate; they become flabby, soft and out of condition, and possibly lose that which they have built up. But if they obey the inward urge, they will keep on and seek ever more difficult enterprises which will test their mettle: keep them strong, and still further strengthen their character. They will also be wise if they see to it that the best things of life are not neglected altogether. Let each find time for the finer and richer things which money cannot buy.

Granted that a businessperson such as this misses many of the best things of life, yet what a difference in character is there between them and the drifter, the man or woman of no ambition. They are like a granite rock compared with the mud heap, or a steamship contrasted with a floating log.

It is true that a fortune is, in itself, not worth winning, it brings more trouble than happiness, but the character-building effect of striving for it are valuable beyond estimation.

Success, however, is not confined to business, for there are the professions. To achieve success in a profession demands the same qualities of character as does a business career. There are the same or similar difficulties to be overcome, such as lack of recognition, prejudice, jealousy, lack of clients, shortage of money. These call out the best in a man or woman: steadfastness, patience, perseverance, faith, courage, hope, vision. They test the aspirant to fame in almost every direction, and who can say how great the character-building effect may be!

Again, it is not everyone who can follow either a professional or business career. There is the bookkeeper, the mechanic, the mother or father in the home. Within all of these, as in all human beings, is the divine urge calling them to nobler effort, loftier aims, higher service, more perfect expression. To everyone the path of success lies open. Everyone can improve, can strive, can develop talents, do better work in the world, serve his or her fellows and thus build up character. The mother can become a better mother to her children, and a more competent home manager. She can improve her mind, develop her talents and increase her efficiency. By so doing she will serve better, be a greater blessing, and build up her own character. The "helpless critter" can overcome her helplessness. The muddler can introduce order into her home, and method into her work. The indolent can become industrious. The bookkeeper can become a better bookkeeper, the blacksmith can become a better blacksmith. Each can increase their knowledge in other directions, thus preparing themselves for higher posts and greater responsibilities in the future. This entails effort and striving; it brings out good qualities, it builds up character.

Success and character-building go hand in hand. The greatest object of life is the building of character, and character is the only thing that we can take with us when we depart. The greatest thing about success is that it builds character.

I have said that we must all be successful, that we must all press towards the mark, all seek after the prize. I am reminded of the blind, what of them? They, too, can overcome. They can rise superior to their disability and serve life and humanity in faithful work, as indeed, they are already doing. Through this they are building better, probably, than they know.

Again, I am reminded of one who lies helpless and paralysed with a broken back, broken for us in the Great War. What of him? He, too, has overcome. He, too, is successful. He, in teaching us patience in suffering, has done all that life asks of him. He, too, has built up character.

It will be seen, then, that we must all aspire, all overcome difficulty, climb to higher things, expressing more perfectly that "something" within us which is the inherent perfection of the divine idea. We must all follow the gleam, all "hitch our wagon to a star", all press after higher ideals. Some are called to great responsibility, some to great sacrifice and noble service, other still less strenuous and more peaceful avocations, but all of us are called to overcome, to strive, to make good, to master our weaknesses, to give better service, to better our work, to improve our minds, to express ourselves more perfectly, and, above all, to build up character.

Chapter Three

The Mental and Spiritual Causes of Success

Although success in life has to be accomplished by effort and action, this outward striving is only the visible part of the complete process of achievement. There is an inner and outer side to everything, and, in the case of successful achievement, the inner, although useless without the outer, is the more important. There is an inner world of "cause", and the outer life is its effect. If the "cause" of our life is at fault it is little that we can do in the outer life to correct it. Indeed, it is impossible, no matter how we strive, to alter in the outer life of effect that which is due to wrong work in the world of cause. First in the unseen, then in the seen - this is the law. "Whatsoever a man soweth, that shall he also reap". All is cause and effect. What you sow in your thought-world you reap in your outer life. You reap success or failure outwardly according to what you create inwardly. It is useless striving to achieve success in outward affairs if the inner life is working against you. He that is not for me is against me, said the great one, and this is true of the mind. If it is not working for you, it is working hard against you. No one can succeed if their subconscious mind is doing its best to produce failure. "A Kingdom divided against itself cannot stand", and before successful achievement becomes possible there must be harmonious agreement between the two worlds of action, the inner and the outer.

There are thousands who are striving in the outer world of effect without success. No matter how they labour and persevere they can never get going. Their desire for success is very strong: they want to accomplish something worthwhile: they long to lift themselves and their family into a better position: they dream of rising to a position of greater responsibility, yet all in vain, for their attempts are abortive: there is some influence which checkmates every effort.

This influence is that of the subconscious mind. Astrological readers will object and say that it is due to planetary influence. Others will say that it is karma. If either is, or both are true, this does not alter the fact that in the subconscious mind we have the active source of the trouble, and it is only by altering the subconscious mind that we can become free. Just as some people inherit a tendency to disease, and their whole life is a long, drawn-out battle against sickness, so also are there those who inherit a tendency to fail, and unless some radical change is effected, nothing but failure will be expressed in the life.

There are also those who are born healthy and strong, and no matter what they do they enjoy perfect health from the cradle to the grave. There are also those who are born to success, and there is nothing on earth that can stop them from succeeding. If, through imprudence, they lose everything they have, and have to start life afresh, it does not daunt them. Soon they are forging ahead again, and, profiting by experience, they achieve an even greater success than before.

I have made a hobby of conversing with successful people in many walks and stations of life and has found that they all possess the same type of mind. There is the same mental outlook, and, in varying degrees, the same confidence, the same faith and strength of character, the same directness, the same courage, decision and action. Also, in those occupying the highest positions, such as business magnates, great financiers and captains of industry, there is splendid judgement and a sense of solidity and power. But in all there is the same mental outlook, the same serene confidence, no matter what their position might be. It is found as much in a successful shopkeeper in a small town, or even a successful costermonger, as in the great ones of the earth.

I have also made a practise of conversing with tramps and vagabonds, and have found them all possessed of a certain type of mind. Just as the successful exude success, so do these poor fellows exude failure. Their whole outlook on life is eloquent of failure, disappointment, lack of achievement.

I have already said that the cause of disease and failure is in the subconscious mind. It does not matter what theory we believe in as to fate, Karma, or planetary influence; the fact remains that the active cause of disease and failure is in the subconscious mind.

We each inherit a certain type of subconscious mind. Let us see what is the effect. The body, right from the commencement of the physical life, is constructed by the subconscious mind. It may build a strong body or a weak one: one full of health and vigour or one ailing and full of disease. In each case it is the work of the subconscious mind. During the life the strong, healthy body, produced by one type of mind, will be entirely free from disease, simply because the subconscious mind has no desire to produce disease and no intention of doing so. On the other hand, the other type of subconscious mind, having produced a weak body, thinks it necessary to produce disease, and, according to its ideas, disease is produced. Disease does not come of itself. Disease is the expression of erroneous ideas in the subconscious mind. The subconscious mind is a wonderful and extraordinary intelligence which has charge of every cell in the body. Every disease that is produced has its matrix in the thought and intention of the subconscious mind.

Not only has the subconscious mind complete control (subject, of course, to a higher power and higher laws) over the body, but it also controls the life, except insofar as it is influenced by conscious thought and suggestion. The outward life is a reflection or outward expression of the inward life, just as, in the same way, the body is the outward expression of the mind. One type of subconscious mind will produce success unlimited, while another type will just as surely produce failure. It all depends upon the kind of subconscious mind.

Believers in a hopeless fate, if any such should see these words, which is doubtful, will say at this point that if this is the case then nothing can be done! They have inherited the wrong type of subconscious mind; therefore, they cannot be anything else but a failure.

This is, however, where we part company. I believe in fate, but only as *something to be overcome*. The reason why one person should inherit a health or success type of subconscious mind, and another a disease or failure type of subconscious mind, does not come within the scope of this book. Sufficient to say here, that life is not a pleasure trip, and the greatest privilege we have is the overcoming of hereditary weaknesses and failings. One who has inherited the failure or lack of success type of mind, has the great privilege of overcoming it. When a person has overcome, they will realise what a great blessing their seeming disadvantage has been in the building up of character. Character building is the great thing for which we are here, and there is nothing that builds up character more than the long struggle, *not with poverty or failure, but with the inherited causes of failure, which are deeply embedded in the subconscious mind*.

Psychologists will tell you that it is your conscious thinking that influences the subconscious mind. You might think from this that the subconscious mind is a dull, inert thing, incapable of doing any thinking on its own account. On the contrary, it is capable of a quality of logical thinking that far exceeds our powers of conscious thought. Not only so, but it is always thinking, and never rests. It is this perpetual thinking on the part of our subconscious minds that almost entirely controls our lives.

This subconscious thinking is a very real thing. If this mind is pulling one way, and the conscious mind the other, is it any wonder that, in spite of strenuous effort, failure results? It is powerful: it is incessant: it is insistent. It creates vibrations that either attack or drive away success.

It is not easy to alter the subconscious mind. It takes more than a few affirmations of success and bright hopes to change the outlook, understanding and intention of this great giant - yet it can be done.

I have said that the subconscious mind is influenced by the conscious thinking of the objective mind. This is true. I have also often said that the thoughts which we allow to sink down into the subconscious mind act as suggestions upon which the subconscious mind acts. This, too, is true. There is, however, a much more powerful factor, which is, that the majority of our thoughts come to us from the subconscious. What actually happens is that instead of us using suggestion to our subconscious mind, our subconscious mind uses suggestion on us and controls our life through suggestion. Therefore, unless we master it, it is the subconscious which manages the life and not we ourselves. It was James Allen who said: "The essential difference between a wise man and a fool is that the wise man controls his thinking, the fool is controlled by it." This is a true saying, for unless we can transmute our thoughts, they will control us and drive us, not where we would desire to go, but in the way that fate and our subconscious mind would have us go.

From the subconscious wells up a constant stream of thoughts, which rises into consciousness. If these thoughts are strong and positive they will urge us on to victory, success and achievement. If, however, we have inherited a negative type of mind, then the thoughts will be tinged with fear and indecision, and unless they are altered will assuredly block the path to success.

From, or through, the subconscious mind of the successful type of person rises a constant stream of virile, courageous thoughts: of action, decision, resolution, power. This mind will urge its owner onto success and achievement. There will be no hesitation, weakness or a resolution, no giving into fate, no giving up in despair. The greater the difficulty the more strength will such a mind display. The subconscious mind, in any case, is untiring, inexhaustible, containing limitless powers. How important is it, then, that it should be helping instead of retarding the life.

From the subconscious mind of the unsuccessful type rises a constant stream of failure thoughts: thoughts of weakness, irresolution, fear, lack of confidence, indecision. When the unfortunate man would otherwise succeed, all his efforts are check-mated, and his resolution weakened by the untiring, unceasing efforts of this inner mind.

There is a dominant note in every subconscious mind. This dominant note controls the life. If it is one of courage, confidence, decision, action: in other words, if it is the success type, then success must follow just as surely as day follows night.

On the other hand, if the dominant note is one of fear, lack of self-confidence, of accusation and hesitancy; in other words, the failure type, then success will be impossible.

Those who believe in fate and control from outside sources, will say that failure is due to influences and vibrations which surround one's pathway in life. This is perfectly true, but it depends on ourselves as to whether we respond to these vibrations and influences. We have inherited or brought with us, a mind of a certain type, and this is the extent of fate and predestination. All that we have to overcome is the wrong dominant note in our subconscious mind. It is this note of vibration which attracts either opportunity or difficulty, according to its kind. The outward life is the effect of this dominant note in the subconscious mind. This inner world of thought is "'cause" and the outer life is merely "effect". According to the dominant note of your inner mind so shall your life be.

This dominant note forms the centre around which the life revolves. Whatever that centre may be, is reflected in the whole of life. If it is success, achievement, action, confidence, abundance, then the whole life will reflect success, achievement and prosperity. Opportunities will come unsought: indeed, so many avenues will open up, it will be difficult to make a choice. If, on the contrary, the centre is made-up of a firmly seated belief in failure, of hesitancy, fear, lack, limitation, then the whole life will exhibit failure, lack of achievement, weakness and poverty.

If the source of all weakness, failure, and lack of achievement is in the subconscious mind; if the dominant note of this inner mind is the determining factor in one's life, how is it possible to alter this dominant note or attitude? Before answering this question, it must be pointed out that the great task before anyone who seeks to succeed and achieve, who, up to the present has failed or only partly succeeded in life, is not the overcoming of failure itself, but of those causes within which produce failure. Before we can grapple with "effects" we must first deal with causes. "First within and then without", this is the law.

The dominant note of the subconscious mind can be changed, in course of time, by a process of patient transmutation of thought. The will and the conscious mind must act together and perform the duties of a transforming station. As the stream of thought rises into consciousness it must be transformed or transmuted, and thus altered in character. Each thought must be polarised from negative to positive. Every sight seen, sound heard, or article read, which suggests to us failure or lack of achievement, must be "reversed" also. The consequence of this will be that all thoughts rising up from the subconscious will be transmuted, and all thoughts suggested by sights, sounds, experiences and reading, will be reversed also, thus producing a constant stream of positive, polarised thought to flow back into the subconscious mind. In this way the subconscious mind can be re-educated. In time, it becomes entirely changed. It is a slow process, but it is sure, for the effects of right thinking are cumulative. As the subconscious mind becomes changed so does the outer life become transformed by the renewing of the mind.

In our next lesson this subject of re-educating the subconscious will be dealt with more fully, and further methods described. In the meantime, will you grasp the following: -

(1). The cause of all your failures, troubles and difficulties is contained within yourself. Circumstances have no power over you; they are but a reflection of your inner thought life.

(2) Therefore, what you have to do in order to overcome circumstances, is to overcome yourself, or, rather, your subconscious mind.

(3) This can be accomplished by transmuting every negative thought into its positive opposite.

Appendix

In this chapter, all the blame has been laid on the subconscious mind. This has been done for the sake of simplicity, but is not, strictly speaking, correct. The actual cause of the failure impulses and timid thoughts which rise into consciousness is the character of the personality. We bring ourselves or real, inward character, with us, and "inherit" a body and physical "outfit", which corresponds with what we are, or which provides us with the best kind of experience for our development. Further, we are not thinkers so much as receivers of thoughts which rise into consciousness via the subconscious. These thoughts are doubtless changed in character or given a bias according to the nature of the dominant note of the subconscious. If this note is one of failure, timidity and pessimism, then all thoughts and impulses will be of this character, and will, unless corrected, result in actions which cannot fail to produce failure in the life. On the other hand, if the dominant note is of the success, overcoming, courage, steadfastness, optimism type, then actions are produced that must lead to success and achievement. This raises the tremendous and fascinating question why one should bring with him into this life a personality and inner character that is weak and vacillating, and another should bring with him a personality that is strong and steadfast. This subject, however, does not come within the scope of this little book. I have dealt with it more fully elsewhere.[1]

---

1. "The Path of Victory" a leaflet published by Henry Thomas Hamblin.

Chapter Four

Vision and Mental Imagery

Not only must there be a reversal into its positive opposite of all negative thoughts, there must also be definite constructive thinking aiming at a definite goal. Everything that has ever been accomplished in this world has been done by constructive thinking. Before a river can be bridged, or a desert irrigated, the bridge or irrigation scheme has to be thought out, by constructive thinking, in the mind of its originator. Outward achievement is always preceded by interior vision. First in the unseen, then in the seen, this is the law of creation. It does not matter whether the desired achievement is the building of a giant dam or tidying up of the home: the law is the same and has to be obeyed. In each case the desired result must be visualised and then constructively worked out, first in thought and then in physical action. The two modes of action cannot be separated: one is incomplete without the other. First, mental action - then physical. First, creative cause - then objective effect.

We are, all of us, continually dealing with immutable law and creative cosmic forces. The law never alters, and creative forces never cease to operate. We are either misusing these immense things to produce failure, or we are constructively using them to produce success. If we use our minds destructively, we attract to us every possible element of failure; whereas if we use our minds constructively, we actually increase our own powers, and at the same time, attract to us the materials and opportunities out of which we can construct success. It is of the utmost importance that we should understand the mental and spiritual laws of creative action.

The difference between people of great achievement and those who never rise above mediocrity, is one of vision and constructive thought. The ordinary person does not think constructively, see possibilities or visualise them. The greatest statesmen, generals, inventors and leaders have been men and women of large vision. Without their vision they would have been nonentities. That such people were born for their part and were especially endowed is no doubt true, but all of us in humbler spheres of service can exercise the same faculties; can obey the same law and use the same creative forces. How high we may ultimately find ourselves does not matter; sufficient, at this stage, that we are climbing. There is no "marking time" stage: we are either advancing or slipping back. We must go forward, every one of us: we must all be successful in something, but what that something is is immaterial so long as we make progress. Life is progress and ever-increasing expression. We must go forward, otherwise we work against the laws of life.

Vision operates in two ways. First, it has a corrective and educative effect upon the subconscious mind. Second, it attracts to itself, in the outer world, the material for its own objective expression. There is nothing wonderful or magic about this faculty, for everyone uses it to a greater or less degree. Successful people are always visualising success, whereas unsuccessful people visualise their own failure. Each gets, in his outward life, a result corresponding to the nature of his vision. For instance, a woman with a successful type of mind has, we will suppose, a small business. Her mind, however, is larger than her business, and she senses the possibilities which lie ahead and constantly thinks in terms of "big business", and sees, in her mind's eye, the expansion which afterwards takes place. On the other hand, one with a negative and pessimistic type of mind, sees no big business in front of him. He is filled with fear, mentally picturing failure, and is forever fearing his own bankruptcy, thus hurrying himself along the path of disaster. It is in our own thoughts and mental picturing that success or failure lie. These are the creative causes of which the outward life is but the effect.

Before a bridge can be built it has to be visualised in its constructor's mind. All the difficulties of the undertaking have to be visualised and overcome, first in the mind picture, and later on the drawing board. The success of the undertaking is visualised right from the commencement. Difficulties are no sooner found than all the resources of constructive, creative imagination are brought to bear on the problem until a solution is found. There is not a thought of ultimate failure: there is no dread or fear of the difficulties of the tasks: there is, instead, perfect confidence in ultimate success, and a keen delight in overcoming difficulties. This is the way in which great achievements are wrought, first in the mind by constructive thinking and vision, and later by actual physical work in steel and stone. This shows the mode of action which takes place in the mind of a typically successful person. It will be seen that the mental work is of the greater importance. No matter how perfect the machinery, if the designing mind is at fault the complete bridge will never materialise. If the head of the project fears and doubts, if his mental pictures are those of failure: if he dreads difficulties, the bridge can never be completed. This successful achievement of any work, great or small, depends upon the thoughts and mental pictures of the originating and executive mind. It is his thoughts, his mental pictures, his strength of character that carries the project to a successful issue, and all the hundreds or thousands of men employed all do their part according to the mental pictures and thoughts in the mind of the originator of the enterprise. If his mind wobbles then the bridge will wobble, and finally never be built at all.

What is true of large enterprises is true of every undertaking, no matter how small or insignificant it may be. If a man has a business and his mind wobbles, then his business will wobble also, and finally be closed down. If his business is to succeed, he must have a steadfast mind. His business will be a perfect reflection and indication of the state of his thoughts and mental pictures; therefore, in order to succeed, his mind must be stable, creating only those pictures which visualise successful achievement. What is held in the mind becomes translated into the outer life: unconsciously every action is affected by the thoughts and mental picturing. Picture failure, difficulties and troubles, and these are bound to manifest in the life. It is not realised by those who are afflicted in this way how utterly their minds are soaked in pessimism, fear, dread and failure. Fear, worry, doubt, apprehension, these effectually bar the road to success by taking away willpower, firmness, decision and ability to seize golden opportunities as they arise. Let an unsuccessful person examine his or her mind, mental pictures and thoughts, and what will he or she find? It will be found that he or she pictures everything from the failure point of view. If it is a tiny business, then, instead of a big business being constantly visualised, visions of non-payment of rent, overdue accounts, and possible closing down of the business are held in the mind. Every difficulty is looked forward to with dread, and, in spite of gifts and talents, there is no confidence in his or her abilities. Such people will not sit for examinations because they fear they will fail. They have the ability to pass, but their mental pictures and negative thoughts take away all their self-confidence. Thus, do thousands, through lack of knowledge, become failures in life, because of entertaining mental pictures and thoughts which tend to drag them down.

I have already pointed out that vision or mental picturing affects the subconscious mind. This is, however, in addition to, or in conjunction with, the reversal of every negative thought into its positive opposite. Thought reversal must continually be practised, and, with it, picture reversal as well. The gloomy pictures of pessimism, failure and despair, must be replaced by those of optimism, success and achievements. Not, by the way, the silly optimism that drifts along, weakly refusing to look unpleasant facts in the face; but the robust optimism and confidence that will "face the music" and overcome difficulties by right action instead of relying upon pious hopes.

By thought reversal and by replacing the vision of failure by that of victorious achievement, the impulses from the subconscious mind gradually become changed. Instead of being weak and hesitating, the impulse is towards strength and decision. The character and conduct also change: the former becomes robust: the latter directed to, and concentrated upon, a definite aim.

Thought and mental picture reversal is not easy, but it is possible. I have done it, and so can you. I am a born negative thinker, who has won his way up out of the depths. I have climbed from poverty, inefficiency, failure and despair to know all the joys of achievement. I have learned to overcome worry, care, fear and pessimism. I have raised myself out of the horrible pit of chronic ill health and untold suffering. I have changed from being a "hanger-on" to others to be a leader, and I tell you here, that it has been done mainly and largely through belief in the power within me: through turning every negative thought and mental picture into its positive opposite and visualising an ideal and pursuing it.

I have had to examine my thoughts and mode of thinking: to find in what subjects my thoughts ran in negative channels: to find also and visualise their exact opposites. It has been necessary to watch my thoughts and seize hold of each offender and deliberately conjure up a bright picture exactly opposite in character. What man has done, man can do. It does not matter how hopeless, inefficient, pessimistic, weak, fearing or negative one may be, the way of escape is open to those who aspire to a higher and better life of achievement and overcoming. To such a one I say: "Leave off fighting life and learn instead to conquer yourself and overcome your own weaknesses of character". This can only be done by reversing your thoughts and mental pictures, holding the vision in your mind of an ideal life to which you long to attain.

Hold the vision in your mind of all that you hope to be, and patiently reverse every negative thought and picture, until at last you think in the same way that a successful person of action and achievement thinks. When this becomes a habit, your life will begin to change, for thoughts and mental imagery become translated into action, and actions build up the life. A successful person does not think or visualise in the way they do because they are successful, but they are successful because of the way they think and visualise. Alter your thoughts and mental pictures, and you transform your life.

Chapter Five

Use Your Imagination

At one time practical people and men of affairs looked askance at the imagination. Such is not the case today, for they know that nothing has ever been accomplished yet without the use of the imagination. Just as the whole universe has been imaged in the Cosmic Imagination, so also all man's achievements have first to be imaged in the human mind.

The imagination is the greatest power of the human mind: it is possessed by all but is used correctly only by the few. Those who wish to succeed must learn to develop and use this wonderful faculty.

The imagination is the creative faculty of mind. In the Infinite Cosmic Imagination, the Universe has been imaged and brought into being. In the same manner man, in his finite imagination, creates for himself his outward circumstances. He does not create from nothing, but forms and moulds pictures out of mind stuff (call it psychic or astral substance if you prefer). What you create in this way will endeavour to manifest in your life, but it needs work, industry and intelligent effort to bring it to fruition. By the use or misuse of this wonderful imaginative faculty, man either builds up his life in the form of true success and achievement or breaks it down into failure and despair. In addition, the right use of the creative imaginative mind greatly increases efficiency. It strengthens and improves the mind in every direction, and also increases mental activity, without which ideas can never be converted into action and action into successful achievement.

Endeavour always to visualise every problem which confronts you. In your imagination picture the whole matter in its entirety, and trace, in every direction, the probable results of various types of action and methods of dealing with the difficulty.

When you are receiving instructions, visualise everything that is said to you. Compel your mind to form mental pictures of everything that is said to you, and, if you cannot do so, ask questions until you receive such additional information as shall enable you to complete the picture.

Visualise, also, everything that you wish to remember. See every detail in your mind's eye before dismissing it to the subconscious.

Use your imagination in your work and play. In your work get your imagination to play round it. Endeavour to grasp the whole difficulty with a clear, alert mind, and then see how easy it becomes. If it is mechanical or artistic work "see" it accomplished better than it has ever been done before, and each day do your work a little better and with more grace, deftness and expedition. In your play visualise your stroke and put yourself into it, so to speak, and thus improve your accuracy.

Visualise your ideals. Hold before you constantly a mental picture of that which you hope to be, or of that which you desire to achieve. Do not, however, use this power in an occult way in order to force certain things to manifest in your outward life by willpower and demand. Instead of this, simply visualise your desired achievement so as to focus your energies and inner forces in such a way as to make a real, honest achievement in the practical affairs of everyday life possible.

One who will practise along these lines will increase their efficiency very considerably. Their mental powers will be greatly strengthened, and concentration largely increased. In the course of time they become capable of directing the powers of their minds, like a focused beam of light, upon any subject for as long as is necessary, and then to dismiss the matter entirely and turn their attention to other matters.

Further, they will be able to grasp a problem in its entirety and suggest many courses of action. They can do this because they possess developed powers of imagination, concentration, and clear, logical and connected thinking.

Chapter Six

Overcoming Circumstances

By thought control and mental imagery of the right kind, a belief in our power to overcome and succeed gradually develops and becomes established. By degrees there dawns a new inward power. This is the power of the real I AM, which is the real self. Instead of thinking and worrying with the surface mind, endeavouring to achieve through the finite will, we begin to use the whole of our mind, realising that behind us we have omnipotent power.

He who realises the greatness of his subconscious mind and thinks deeply with the power of his whole mind, becomes a force with which to be reckoned. When to this he adds a realisation of the power of the Spirit, there are no difficulties which he cannot overcome. The power within is greater far than any difficulty, for it is spiritual, and "nought can stand before thy Spirit's force".

It does not matter what our position in life may be, nor how unfavourable our circumstances, we can rise above them, for the power within us is infinite. So long as we let circumstances and environment master us, we are slaves. When, however, we become bigger than our circumstances, our environment alters accordingly. People often say to me: "If only my circumstances were different, I could get on". They are surprised when they are told that if their circumstances were made easier their troubles would not be less, but greater. Our circumstances are always the best for us at the time, and the most suitable for our development. The object of life is character development, and our circumstances are always those which will develop us in the best possible way. If our life and environment are petty, then we must become broader and bigger in character before they can be changed. What is the difference between a person of great achievement and a struggling little tradesman in a back street? Is it circumstances and environment? If they changed places, would they remain in the same position and environment for long? No, the difference is in the individual.

It is not environment or circumstances which have to be changed, but the person's thinking. If a man is in poverty and difficulty, he cannot overcome them by fighting them - some, indeed, spend their whole life in fighting difficulty, and without success - he can overcome them only by altering and changing *himself*. The real fundamental difference between successful and unsuccessful people is this: the former always looks to herself for the causes of her failure and alters herself and her methods in the light of experience, while the latter blames circumstances for his lack of success, and, instead of altering himself, endeavours to change his circumstances by fighting them.

A "big" person will always readily admit that their temporary failure - for all fail at times, and a successful person is one who learns from failure - is due to them alone. They learn wisdom from every set-back and grows "bigger" in consequence.

The outward life is a reflection of the life within. Our circumstances are an effect and not a cause. The cause of our circumstances is in ourselves. The unsuccessful ones are forever blaming circumstances for their troubles, and, by so doing, allow their environment to have tremendous sway over their lives.

Before we can escape from unfavourable circumstances, we must outgrow them. Our environment always harmonises with our inward mental state, and when we alter within, we are quickly raised to better circumstances. Before we can be successful, we must merit success. Before we can achieve, we must develop the power to achieve. Before we can fill a higher and bigger position, we must make ourselves capable, and more than capable, of filling it.

This law is merciless. If, by some freak of fortune, a person suddenly becomes wealthy without being ready for it, there follows the most disastrous results. During the war many people who otherwise would not have been successful, were able, under the peculiar conditions then obtaining, and in the absence of competition, to make a fortune. The results can be imagined. They paraded their wealth in a vulgar manner, were avoided by cultured people, and lost the friendship of their old friends. Having no culture they did not know what to do, either with themselves or their money. My under-gardener, who became a tank sergeant during the war, was employed afterwards as a chauffeur by a new-rich couple. He had to leave his situation: he could stand the army and the Great War, but he could not endure the life they led him. They were drunken, unhappy, quarrelsome, overbearing, and without consideration. The life they lived was like that of the underworld. Their wealth was a terrible curse instead of a blessing. The law is always working. We can occupy a higher position only when we are ready for it.

In contrast to this case, there are those who have climbed rapidly, by sheer worth, from the lowest poverty to extreme wealth, and have filled their new position with dignity and grace. These were ready for their rise: they grew bigger than their circumstances, and when they moved to higher positions were ready to fill them with honour.

There has been a great deal of teaching of recent years, promising a golden fortune to those who will follow certain methods of mind domination. This is ancient black magic in a new guise. You have to visualise a certain sum of money for a certain time each day and will it to come to you. Nothing is said about earning it or giving service in exchange for it or being worthy of it - you simply demand it and will that it shall be yours. The theory is that if your desire is strong enough you can sit with folded arms, and the desired wealth drops into your lap. Fortunately, it does not, as a rule, work, and its devotees are thus saved from disaster and suffering. Those who can force wealth to come to them in this way have ample cause bitterly to regret it. Such methods are against the laws of life and true progress. The only true success is through service. Endeavouring to get something for nothing leads to suffering and disaster.

The power within, then, must be used not to fight unpleasant surroundings, but to increase our worth, improve our service, extend our efficiency and enlarge our capacity. This applies to both men and women in all ranks of life. It is as applicable to the mother who stays at home to look after young children as to the man of business: it applies equally to the woman of independent means and the man of affairs or the factory hand. No matter what the position in life may be, circumstances can be overcome only from within, and life cannot be made a success by making it easier, even if such a thing is possible.

Life is a stern experience, and its discipline cannot be avoided. All attempts to dodge its tasks and lessons are ultimately defeated. The avoidance of life's duties is the cause of untold suffering. Life insists upon the lesson being learned, and if it is not learned willingly it has to be learned through painful experience. The unthinking imagine that the object of life is to have a good time. Because of this they constantly seek to avoid life's discipline, and to choose the easier path. They wonder why it is that life becomes increasingly difficult. They are not aware that it is merely the law compelling them to learn their lesson through suffering instead of through voluntary self-improvement.

It was Philip Brooks who said: "Do not pray for easy lives: pray to be stronger men. Do not pray for tasks equal to your powers: pray for powers equal to your tasks".[1]

No truer or more faithful words were ever uttered. It is impossible either to avoid the discipline of life or to make life easy. The only way is to become greater than our difficulties, bigger than our environment and master of our own weaknesses.

A simple and homely illustration will explain what I mean with regard to mastering our own weaknesses. We will take the case of a man who is not doing well in his place of employment. He is not liked by the management because he frequently arrives late, because his health and temper are not good, because his work is not quite as good as it might be. Other men are promoted over his head. They are not cleverer than he, but they are more punctual, more dependable, are fitter in health and better tempered; their work, also, is a little better than his. What is the cause of the whole trouble, and how can it be remedied? The sole cause is a weakness of character. He lacks self-control and cannot rise in the morning at the proper time. He lies in bed until the position becomes desperate, then dashes through his ablutions, snatches a hasty breakfast and dashes to the station. Even if he gets his train he arrives at his

---

1. Reverend Phillips Brooks (1835-1893) was an American Episcopal clergyman renowned as a preacher. https://www.britannica.com/biography/Phillips-Brooks

office with nerves in a fearful jangle, his digestion upset and quite unfit for his work. Sometimes he may miss his train, arriving at the office late and receiving a well-merited rebuke. It is only a matter of time, and this man will be discharged. All his failings and shortcomings, as well as his good points, are carefully noted by his superiors, and unless he improves, the time must come when he will lose his position.

How can this man put the whole matter right? Simply by correcting his weakness of character. When he has overcome his weakness he will rise early, bath, exercise and dress in comfort. Descend to breakfast at his leisure, and stroll to the station in good time for his train. When he arrives at the office he will be fit and well and capable of working at the top of his ability.

This homely illustration will show how by altering *ourselves* and improving our own *character*, we can overcome the difficulties of life and become successful instead of a comparative failure.

This self-improvement and inward growth which makes one bigger than one's circumstances, and raises one in the scale of achievement, can be accomplished in two ways. First by willpower, brute force and frontal attacks, or second, by the realisation and right use of the power within. The first method is exhausting, and, although successful in some cases, more often results in failure, for the more we fight our weaknesses the stronger they seem to become. The second method is infallible, for the power within is infinite. This power is spiritual and is not to be used to dominate and influence other people, but to build up one's own character: to increase one's efficiency and usefulness: to make one more capable, steadfast, reliable: more fitted to fill our higher position and to bear the larger responsibilities of life and citizenship.

The power within us is limitless but lies dormant and unexpressed. It can be brought into expression only as we become enlarged in character, broadened in thought, greater in our ideas, and more lofty in our ambitions.

CHAPTER SEVEN

Opportunity

It is the complaint of the unsuccessful that they have never had opportunities such as those enjoyed by other people. "Opportunity makes the man", they cry. "We have had no opportunities therefore we are failures, and the fault is not ours". They explain the success of others as being the result of luck or opportunity. They think that success is in circumstances and opportunity, not realising that everything is in the man himself.

It is said that fortune knocks at every man's door once in a lifetime, but I would go further and say that innumerable opportunities are constantly coming to man, but, for the most part, he does not recognise them. One of the differences between the successful and the unsuccessful is that the former recognise opportunity and realise the immense number of chances which come their way, while the latter are blind to them.

It has been said that adopting the right attitude of mind brings opportunity to one through the law of attraction. It was Henry Harrison Brown who taught the "dollars want me", as opposed to the "I want the dollars" attitude of mind, and his teaching, strange though it may seem to some, is perfectly sound.[1]

All are familiar with the peculiarity of memory: if we cannot recall a certain fact to mind, the more we try to remember it the more it eludes us; yet, if we leave off trying to remember, the missing fact comes into consciousness unbidden. It is the same with fortune, for she is a fickle jade, and the more we pursue her the more she eludes us: yet, if we cease to chase her, she will come and fawn at our feet. There are cases on record of men who have followed after material success in vain for years, not for their own sake so much as for others dependent on them. When those for whom they sought success were dead, and fortune was no longer desired or sought after, great success came unbidden. This is always being put down to the perverseness of life, but I believe it is due to a mental law. When

---

1. Henry Harrison Brown (1840-1918) was an early New Thought author and spiritualist. His books include: *New Thought Primer, Origin, History and Principles of the Movement* (1903), *How to Control Fate Through Suggestion* (1906), *Not Hypnotism but Suggestion* (1906), *Psychometry* (1906), and *Dollars Want Me* (1917).https://en.wikipedia.org/wiki/Henry_Harrison_Brown

you try to go to sleep you cannot, yet when you do not care a straw whether you sleep or not you fall off without knowing it. It is all the action of the same law. If you strive anxiously after success the vibrations of your mind keep it away, but when you confidently believe that success wants you, it is attracted to you.

Another way in which a correct mental attitude helps is by enabling one to recognise opportunity when it comes. A man who expects success to come his way is on the lookout for opportunity, and when it comes is ready to seize it with both hands. On the other hand, a pessimist who is quite sure that nothing good can come his way may be surrounded by rich opportunities, and yet will never recognise them or make use of them.

The proper attitude of mind, then, must be, not one of anxious seeking for success, but of calm assurance that success is seeking you. Believe in your heart that opportunity wants you far more than you desire the opportunity. If you possess the right mental attitude men and opportunity will be attracted to you. John Burroughs'[2] words represent this mental attitude perfectly: -

---

2. John Burroughs was an American naturalist, poet, and essayist. He is remembered today as one of the most important **nature writers** of the late 19th and early 20th centuries.

   https://allpoetry.com/John-Burroughs

> "Asleep, awake, by night or day,
> the friends I seek are seeking me".

It is most important to grasp thoroughly this truth that success is seeking you and desires to crown your life. As soon as you fulfil the conditions, success will manifest, simply because it is as natural as health and other forms of good. As soon as we comply with nature's laws of health, health begins to manifest in the body, simply because it is natural to do so. Ill health, being unnatural disappears when the laws of health are observed. In the same way, success is natural, and failure is unnatural. When the conditions are fulfilled, success comes into the life as naturally and easily as the blossoming of a flower. This does not mean that you can afford to be mentally indolent, neither does it mean that you can glide through life, for great mental activity is required and industry and perseverance. But it does mean that when you have fulfilled certain conditions success will crown your life.

Carry the thought strongly in your mind that all good things want you, therefore you have no need to want them. Realise that you are a centre of Cosmic energy, attracting to yourself all the opportunity that you can possibly need or desire. If you do this, you will find so many opportunities coming your way that that you will experience difficulty in making a choice.

When opportunity does come, and you feel sure that it is the right opening that you require, grasp it with both hands. This may lead to many blind alleys and consequent disappointments, but the experience will be valuable, and lessons learned through comparative failure will prepare you for a greater opportunity when it comes.

Never think any failure to be final. No failure is final, and no failure is anything more than a valuable lesson, which, when learned, makes you more experienced and capable of succeeding. Never blame fate: never blame other people: look upon the apparent failure as a valuable experience preparing you for far greater things.

Never look upon any failure as evil. Failures are merely symbols of hidden weaknesses within. Life is infinitely kind, and in each failure is hidden the lessons which must be learned before you can be entrusted with greater things.

Remember also, that he who hesitates is lost, and one who fails to grasp opportunity when it comes his way has the chagrin of seeing it taken by another. No amount of effort after the moment of opportunity has passed can ever bring it back again.

When once an opportunity has gone, do not waste time trying to overtake it, and do not waste valuable time and nervous energy bemoaning your hard fate or bad luck, but look out for another opportunity instead. There is always an opportunity for the one who is ready for it, and who does not dissipate their powers and distract their attention by worrying and fretting over past mistakes and failures.

I said just now that no failure need ever be final. This is true. The only one who can make it final is yourself. Nobody can fail utterly who refuses to be beaten, and nobody can make a success of someone who believes that they are a failure and that it is no use trying anymore. Success or failure is in the mind. What a person believes becomes part of them, and outward circumstances are but symbols of the character within. If you meet with a failure or setback, and believe it to be final, and that you are too old or too weak to make another start, then you will never make another start. By your own belief, you bolt and bar the door of success in your own face.

Let me tell you a true story well within my own experience. There was once a working man, in a fashionable English seaside resort, who saved up enough money to buy a horse and cart. The town was growing fast, much building was going on, and, as a carter, this unlettered son of toil made a huge success. Once a year he had a procession of his horses and carts and a competition for the smartest turn out. The procession was so long and so interesting it was one of the local sights and considered well worth seeing. Success, however, turned the head of this one-time labourer, and, through drink and neglect, the business got into difficulties and had to be sold. The buyers, moreover, alleged certain irregularities, and brought the vendor to court, the result being that he was sent to jail to serve a fairly long service. At this time, our hero, for hero he was, was getting on in years, and the hard prison life broke down his health. When he came out of jail, he was old and broken in health. His face was lined with suffering, mental and physical, ill-health and age. "Ha!" said the wise, shaking their heads, "---- is done for this time: there are no hopes for him". And they had good grounds for their opinion. Old, broken in health, business in the hands of others; character gone; capital all lost; old friends pretending not to see him in the street; could any plight be more hopeless? But that man was not beaten. He was not beaten simply because he was convinced in his own mind that he could rise again, and one who really believes that cannot be kept down for long. What did this man do? Did he go to another town and make a fresh start? Did he hide himself from the people who pointed at him in self-righteous scorn and called him jailbird? No, he stayed in the same town where everybody knew him as a man who had been in prison. He started to "live it down". I have seen him touch his cap to people who pretended not to see him. They were his friends once, but now they do not know him. I have seen his lips tighten a little at a cold rebuff, but he never whined, faltered or complained. The opportunity came for him once again to get one horse and cart, and in spite of his years and infirmities and the opposition arrayed against him, he gradually built up his business again step by step until at last, once again the whole town was dotted with his many horses and carts of every description. Before that man died, he rebuilt his business to its old honourable standing and prosperity, and compelled people to recognise him as a man to be respected and honoured. I take off my hat to this man of humble birth and no education. He was surely sent into this world to teach some of us, with feeble knees, how to be strong. His example has been an inspiration to me when things have tested me and tried me almost past bearing. With this fine man's example before us, can we ever give up in despair? Can we ever accept defeat as final?

Opportunity is knocking at *your* door. If you cannot hear the tapping it is because your mind is slothful. Everyone is surrounded by golden opportunities. What is needed is the mental attitude to attract them closer, the alertness to recognise them, and the action and decision to grasp them. Further, it is necessary to fit oneself for higher and more respectable service. A junior clerk must be capable of filling a head clerk's position, otherwise how can he be promoted? A salesman must be capable of filling a sales manager's position before he can be offered the higher post. A man with a small business must be capable of managing a large one, for, if not, his business can never grow. Always the man must grow before he can fill a higher position.

To sum up. Opportunities in plenty are all around us. We can either attract or repel them, according to our mental attitude. They can be recognised if we look out for them and expect them. Not all of them lead to the success that we aspire to, but, if not, they provide valuable experience. Opportunity must be grasped at the right moment, and it is useless running after it when once it has passed.

Finally, no failure is final. No one need despair. There are as good fish in the sea as ever came out of it. The man who refuses to believe in failure cannot, if he will realise that all cause of failure is within himself, be prevented from succeeding.

Chapter Eight

Success Through Service

It is only in recent years that it has dawned upon humankind that the law underlying success is service. Even now it is imperfectly realised, if at all, by the majority. The unthinking and ignorant still imagine that they can get something for nothing. The thinkers and men of achievement, however, know that there is an underlying law which demands a fair exchange and a square deal. Those who think they can get something for nothing are the ones who get fleeced and swindled by the harpies who batten on the simple and gullible. But, in swindling others, the swindler deceives and cheats himself, for, "behold, God (or the Law of Life) is not mocked, whatsoever a man soweth that shall he also reap". There is a Divine Law of Compensation forever working: with absolute impartiality it rewards us according to our deeds.

It is not denied that there are many who live by their wits and who make money by questionable methods, rendering no service to their fellows. Such, however, are never truly successful: they lead miserable lives: are frequently in trouble, and, more often than not come to a disastrous end. It does not do to judge the lives of such people by merely a few years: it is necessary to view them over a lengthy period. When this is done it is seen how perfectly the Law operates: how, with mathematical exactness, it exacts an eye for an eye and a tooth for a tooth. It must not be overlooked when considering the ease of these harpies who batten on honest yet foolish people, that they are *clever* rogues, and that their apparent or fleeting success is but the shadow of what their real success might have been, and would have been, if they had "run straight".

The great law underlying success cannot be evaded. Many people will admit the working of this law in ordinary simple business transactions, but in complicated modern business, simply because it is so complicated that the working of the law cannot be traced, they deny its power. They think, foolishly, that it can be tricked and avoided, but this is childish, for the law is administered by an Infinite Intelligence.

It is easy to trace the working of the law in simple business transactions. An architect must design a building and supervise its construction before she or he can get paid. The singer has to appear on the stage and sing, or he or she gets no fees. The workman has to do a certain quantity of work before he can draw a certain amount of money. The store has to give the best possible value for money or lose its customers. The dentist has to give satisfaction to her patients or forgo her fee and lose her connection. In all these simple transactions the operation of the law of service and reciprocity is seen to be in action.

However, when we come into complicated business, stocks and shares, luxury trades, and businesses which do nothing more than juggle with figures, the action of the law is not so clearly discerned. This is due simply to the limitations of the human mind. The law continues to work and gives to each exactly that which they deserve.

No matter what the business or profession may be, if it is to continue its existence it must render useful service to the community or a section of the community. It is impossible to point to any successful business which does not render service. The less efficient it is, the less service it renders, and the less successful are its results. The basis of the success of big stores and multiple shops is service. Their form of service is largely one of price; they cannot give personal service such as a small business can, but they can sell more cheaply. The only hope of the small business is personal, individual service. By this means they can render service to a certain section of the public which the big corporation finds it impossible to supply, for there is a class of people who will willingly pay a little more if they can get personal attention. Success, then, in business, either small or large, is based on service.

Individual success is also based on the law of service. So long as we are "in the ruck", neither better nor worse than the next man, our reward is very scanty. We belong to the mass of toilers - to the army of patient drudges. But as soon as we make ourselves more efficient and more original than our fellows; in other words, when we render more conspicuous service, we quickly achieve a most astonishing measure of success.

The surgeon who performs operations more skillfully: the artist who paints more inspired pictures: the engineer who builds better bridges: the actor who acts more perfectly: in fact, anyone who can do something which the world wants, and can do it better than other people, becomes popular, much sought after, and correspondingly successful. This success is due entirely to the law of service. He who serves best obtains the plums of his profession: the prizes of life are literally thrust upon him.

Surgeons and others raise their fees, doubling and quadrupling them, simply in self-defence, and they can hardly be blamed for so doing, although it may seem like profiting by other people's misfortunes. As they point out, there are plenty of other good surgeons whose fees are much lower. It is the same with other callings; only get above the ordinary and in a class by yourself, then, as soon as it becomes known, you will not lack supporters. You can then either serve more, or charge more, according to the amount of love that you have for your fellows.

"He profits most who serves the best" is eternally true. Not merely in money - for many who serve think more of the service than they do of the money - but in other ways, the eternal law works in our lives, bringing us a rich reward in love, harmony and success in exchange for "services rendered". There is a spiritual debit and credit account which is balanced from time to time. The swindlers who live by knocking others down and taking all that they have, saying that it is "good business", wonder why their private life is such a hell of misery, or why their health gives way. They are merely reaping as they have sown. The law of service cannot be broken with impunity: its action can never be evaded.

The age of exploitation is drawing to a close. In the past both the worker and the public have been exploited. It is now being realised that the master must "serve" just as much as the servant; it is being recognised also, by the worker, that the master does serve, and thus has his legitimate place in the scheme of things. Employers also realise today that they have to serve the public as well as their employees. They are recognising the great truth that the better they serve the public the more successful they become, and the more they look after the happiness and welfare of the workers the better the results. Reciprocity, goodwill, service, cooperation - these are the finger-posts to a new era.

Also, the most enlightened in the ranks of labour are beginning to see that their success depends upon their service to the public. They realise that "ca'canny" (slack) methods impoverish the worker instead of enriching him. They are beginning to understand the great underlying law which demands the best efforts of every man. If a man does only half a day's work for a full day's pay, he finds later on that the law of service has worked in such a way as to throw him out of employment. It is the same law that takes away an employer's business if he does not give good value to the public, either in material or service.

It is because business people and others have proved that this law of service is basic, divine and fundamental, that gives hope for the future. The motto of the new age will be: – *"He profits most who serves the best."*

Chapter Nine

Work and Action

Mental action is of paramount importance, but that does not mean that no physical work is necessary. Constructive mental work should lead to a well-directed action. Its object is to focus all the powers of mind and body upon the desired success, thus making achievement possible. Constructive mental action can never take the place of work and honest striving. There is so much erroneous teaching to the contrary that a chapter addressing this subject is necessary.

Those who are seeking success in a wrong manner might be divided roughly into two classes. First, there are those who work and toil too much; who strive continuously in the outer world of effect, leaving no time for reflection. These know nothing of the power of creative thought or the right use of imagination. Toilers such as these become mere automatons - slaves who become worn out before their time. Such can never achieve great or outstanding success, although their patient service meets with its due reward. Second, there are those who, having learned something of the creative powers of mind, wrongly imagine that by merely thinking success they can cause it to drop like a bolt from the blue, right into their laps. My practical readers will think such folly incredible, yet it is true of a great many. There are thousands of foolish and gullible people, who, whilst making no sensible efforts to win success, spend their time and money seeking for a back-stair method which shall make honest striving unnecessary. They fondly imagine that by concentration in the *silence* they can, by a species of witchcraft or magic, get something for nothing – in other words, gain success without either earning it or being deserving of it. Hundreds of books have been written on this type of success, and not one of them has anything to say about work! Comment is unnecessary when it is remembered that the basis of all true success is service. A method which does not improve the individual, thus increasing the value of his or her contribution to the work of the world, can never result in success. Such a method is based on a fallacy: it is in opposition to the laws of life and can result only in failure.

No success has ever been won without action. People of achievement are people of action and decision. They act while other people are merely dreaming and considering. The world is full of impractical dreamers, but the number of those who have both vision and the ability to act promptly and decisively is very small. While it is true that action without vision and imagination can never lead to big results, it is equally true that vision without action produces no results at all.

There are two kinds of action: one is creative, the other executive. Both are necessary. The person who toils and moils without the aid of creative thought and imagination is wrong. On the other hand, those who expect to win success by merely visualising it, sitting with folded hands waiting for a "demonstration", are equally wrong. One, however, who combines both types of action, is right, and his efforts must, sooner or later, result in success.

There is a great difference between idle dreaming and creative imagination. Daydreaming fritters away the mental powers, saps the power of the will and leads to reduced efficiency. Creative thought and imagination, on the contrary, increases one's mental powers, including concentration. The former is mental drifting, the latter is mental action. Action, directed into the right channels, always wins. But even action of this kind must be supplemented by physical action. Having grasped the situation, visualising its possibilities, the next thing is to be up and doing.

One of the outstanding characteristics of successful people is their capacity for work. Not only do they visualise the possibilities of every opportunity; not only do they weigh the matter carefully, deciding whether it is worth grasping or not, they also, as soon as their decision is made, act swiftly and with determination. If they decide to grasp the opportunity they immediately act, and from thence onwards put into their understanding the *whole of their force, energy and power for work*.

Success comes to those who serve best. It is those who build the best bridges, paint the greatest pictures, invent the finest machines, build up the most efficient businesses, who reap the largest success. It is those who can render better service than the average person who can command a better remuneration than the usual. It is those who, in humbler walks of life, do their day's work as well as they possibly can, always striving to do it even better still, who get true satisfaction from life. This success and satisfaction are due to the fact that through work and service they harmonise with Cosmic Law. "It is more blessed to give than to receive", said the Great Teacher, and it is because this is a fundamental truth that true success and satisfaction come to those who serve life and their fellows faithfully and well. It is because the majority of people work on the principle that it is *better to receive than it is to give*, that they reap failure instead of success. For the same reason, those who are successful in money-getting are often failures as far as health and happiness are concerned. These words of the Great Master are absolutely and scientifically true. They expound a deep, fundamental law which underlies success in every department and walk of life. We must first give (serve) before we can receive, and in this giving (serving) we are more blessed than in the receiving. Success, prosperity and the joy of achievement, satisfy for a time, but they soon pall. Of themselves, they bring no lasting satisfaction. In work and service, however, can be found constant happiness and satisfaction, especially if our service is given not so much for what we can get out of it, but as an offering to all humankind. It is because there is more joy in work than there is in its rewards that compels successful people to seek fresh fields to conquer. Their success does not bring them all the happiness that they expected, but they find great joy in work, achievement and the overcoming of difficulty.

It may seem strange that it should be thought necessary to point out such obvious necessities as work, effort and action. Yet it is necessary because of the flood of literature of recent years which teaches that mental power alone is necessary. These writers teach the fundamental error that a person can so use their minds as to compel other people, circumstances and even matter, to conform to their will. I feel sorry for those who follow this teaching, for, while they may apparently succeed for a time, they finally get broken on the wheel of life. Such practices are diametrically opposed to the law of service: they are based on the exact opposite of the divine teaching; therefore, they are bound to fail.

The object of this little book is to present the fundamental laws which underlie all true success. It is the *inner truths* which I wish to teach. The laws which underlie all true achievement are spiritual and immutable. The universe is a big thing: it is maintained by extraordinary powers and laws, and what chance does an individual stand who dares to defy these laws and work against them? The law of service is based on that immutable truth, "it is more blessed (that is, it is really better) to give than to receive". All those, therefore, who go against this law, believing that they can demand, by means of what amounts to nothing less than a perverted form of prayer, giving nothing in return, are pursuing a policy which must end in disaster.

Today, as I write these words, news comes to me that one who for years has followed this policy of making mental demands and using mind domination, has failed. His large business has disappeared; all his plans have miscarried, and he has to start life afresh. It does not surprise me, for one who works along these lines must surely fail. One who considers himself first and his customers or clients last, can never succeed, simply because he goes against the immutable law of service. The successful ones of all ages have been those who, either consciously or unconsciously, have had one object in view, ie: "how best can I serve?"

There is a certain organisation, of a religious character, which claims to do everything by prayer, even to "demonstrating supply", as they call it. Yet, when the leaders of the movement meet together to pray over and discuss the matter of "ways and means", their first concern is, "How can we improve our service to our fellows?". These men and women know the basis of all true success: they know that the law underlying all true prosperity and achievement is that of work and service. They know the value of prayer, or concentration in the silence upon a certain ideal, for this focuses all the scattered mental powers into one powerful beam, bringing all the forces of life to one point. They also know that these focused powers must be applied in service to humankind at large, if success is to be achieved.

To sum up: work and action are of two kinds. First, the creative mental action: the focusing of the mental powers upon one's ideal. Secondly, the use of these "one-pointed" mental powers given freely in service to life and the world.

One of old said: "Beloved, let us love". May I say, in all reverence: "Beloved, let us work and serve", for in work and service do we manifest true practical love.

CHAPTER TEN

Equity, Justice and the Law of the Square Deal

The universe is based upon immutable law. Cosmic law is forever operating, it can never be tricked or evaded. One of the basic laws of the universe is that of justice. If it were not for this principle of absolute justice running through life in its myriad forms, operating all through this infinitely complex universe, the whole Cosmic Scheme would speedily come to grief. It will be admitted, I think, by all my readers, that the Universe could not run successfully - indeed, it could not be carried on at all - without there exists a principle or law of absolute justice which must work with unvarying impartiality always.

What is true of the universe is true also of the life or lives of man. This divine law of justice and impartial compensation is forever acting, and, but for this, chaos would take the place of cosmos, thus making any form of life impossible.

This immutable law upon which the whole structure of the universe depends, cannot be ignored. We may, it is true, both ignore the law and defy it: we may even try, by cunning trickery, to avoid it, but we will suffer accordingly. This is not generally recognised, simply because the effect of wrongdoing is not immediately apparent. Even when it appears it may come in such a form that it is not recognised as a compensating act of the principle of justice. It is true that a man may get rich by sharp practice and dishonest methods, yet, even if he is able to keep his riches, which, very often is not the case, one has only to examine his private life in order to see how perfectly the law operates. He may get riches, true, but his life becomes, in other respects, full of troubles and disasters; all happiness and joy becoming things of the past.

Slowly, the knowledge that all success is grounded upon an undeviating law of justice and square dealing is percolating through to the minds of businessmen and women. The heads of big businesses have for long realised that they must, if their undertakings are to be successful, do a square deal with the public. They know that if they will deal fairly with the public, people will always deal with them. They know that, having once obtained the confidence of the public, this trust must not be betrayed. They are aware of the folly of trading upon their reputation, or of lowering the quality of their goods. They are convinced, because they have proved it, that, as far as dealing with the public is concerned, honesty is the best policy.

They have also, to a lesser extent in some cases, realised that it is also necessary to do a square deal with their employees. They are finding that it pays in hard cash to treat employees with justice and consideration. They are beginning to see that the golden rule is founded upon a law, just as sure in its operation as that of gravitation. When this knowledge becomes more widespread, much greater prosperity, happiness, goodwill and harmony will be the inevitable result.

There are, however, many people, both in business and the professions, who, while admitting that honesty and square dealing "pay" as far as the public and their employees are concerned, still believe that it is "good business" to take advantage of another business or professional man. They think that to crush another when he is down: to take advantage of another's misfortunes, to be harsh and unyielding in a business deal, is both legitimate and profitable. It is, in reality, neither. It may appear, on the surface, to be profitable, but, in the long run, it is not so. The law of justice compensates impartially. At some time and in some way the matter has to be adjusted. Troubles and disasters not connected with business may "square" the matter, or, as is very often the case, people who act in this way find themselves in precisely the same position as their former victims, receiving the same harsh treatment.

This fundamental and universal law of the "square deal" demands of every one of us absolute honesty, integrity, straight methods and sincerity. The affairs of the world at large call for state leaders who are sincere. National affairs demand politicians of high character: not mere opportunists, but people to whom honour and principle are the very breath of life. The welfare of our institutions demands leaders to whom truth and its pursuit are of far greater importance than custom, creed and dogma. Business and the professions are calling for individuals of honour and probity, whose character is built upon honesty, integrity and absolute straightness.

The world needs today, more than ever it has needed in the past, men and women who, while practical and capable, are yet followers of ideals. Such men and women are needed to hold a beacon before the less-evolved; who shall help by their courage, sincerity, integrity and singleness of purpose, to raise humanity to higher and better things.

Let me remind you that mere money-making is not success. True success must embrace every department of life. The most successful are those who build up the highest character, which is reflected into their lives and in all that they do. Money is no good and can bring no happiness if, in order to gain it, you have to sacrifice your ideals, principles and self-respect. Of what use is money if, in the silent watches of the night, when you cannot sleep, voices tell you what an utter failure your life, in reality, is?

True success comes to one who considers honour and principle before self-interest and private gain. It may be a difficult path to tread, but it is the only way to happiness, peace of mind and satisfaction. True success comes to those who will not sacrifice everything upon the altar of their ambition. The wise refuse to sacrifice their health, and do not throw away those precious things which money can never buy; such as love, respect, honour, peace of mind, happiness, and the esteem of their colleagues.

Having watched the careers of many successful and so-called successful people, I can truthfully say that, sooner or later, the law of divine justice and compensation is always seen in operation. All other things being equal, it is the person of probity, honesty, justice and square-dealing who weathers the storms of life. Men and women of great brilliance, who might have had the world at their feet, *had they run straight*, have found their proper level at last. Others, far less brilliant, are occupying high positions, not merely because of their capabilities, but because they can be *trusted and depended upon*.

Never before in the world's history has there been such opportunity for those who have ambition to rise. Those who have "grit" in them can, in this coming New Age, do wonderful things. It is possible for them to rise to positions of great honour, responsibility and usefulness. All the world is at their feet. Fame and fortune are calling for them. It is, however, only those who are "true", who are prepared to live their life to a principle, who need respond. It is only such that the New Age needs. The age of sharp practice and chicanery is passed: the days of sweating and depression, scamped work and time serving, are also passing rapidly away. The New Age demands efficient men and women, but it demands, even more, square dealers.

CHAPTER ELEVEN

Character Building

The only thing that really matters, in this life, is character. If, at the end of this brief journey, we are conscious that our besetting weaknesses have been overcome, then we can die happy; not otherwise. The only thing that we can take with us, when we leave this "training school", is character, and nothing but character. The person who, at the end of his days, has built up and strengthened his or her character, who has put up a good fight in the battle of life, is truly successful. Such people may not be successful according to popular ideas: they may not have amassed wealth or achieved fame, but, if they have built up their character, they have achieved the highest success, for they have won for themselves imperishable riches which can never be taken from them.

Whatever is added to a person's character is added permanently. Character is eternal. In order to add to his or her character, it may be necessary for an individual to meet and overcome tremendous difficulties: to endure patiently grievous losses and disappointments: to experience poignant griefs and sorrows; but the results are worth all the trial and travail, for the value of character is beyond computation; it endures forever while the sufferings and strivings, which produced it, are forgotten. Further, if the lessons have been well learned, the experiences never have to be gone through again. There are, of course, countless experiences for the soul to pass through, for progression is endless, but the experiences which produced character in this life will never have to be gone through again. Character, having been added, makes repetition unnecessary.

Many people complain that their life is simply a succession of troubles. They are no sooner out of one than they are into another. This is not as it should be, for if the soul is progressing normally, learning its lessons as they appear, suffering and happiness should about balance one another. A constant succession of troubles is due to the fact that the lessons of life have not been learned. Until a certain lesson has been learned, or, to put it another way, until a certain weakness of character has been overcome, the difficulty or trouble repeats and persists. This is not due, as was once believed, to someone exterior to the world, plaguing or tormenting man: it is simply the working of the great law of cause and effect. Until this law is recognised man perpetuates troubles for himself.

The inward man or woman, or character, is "cause", and life, circumstances and experiences are "effect". Whatever weakness of character an individual may have, is reflected in his life, experience and circumstances. A man looking at his reflection in a mirror is a good illustration of cause and effect. The man is "cause", his reflection is "effect". If the man is dissatisfied with what he sees in the mirror it is obvious that he himself must change. It is useless for him to complain that the figure he sees is dirty, unshaven and ill-dressed. It is also useless for him to hit the mirror: the only thing to do is to learn the lesson the mirror has to teach him and change himself. Let him shave, wash and clothe himself properly, and the figure in the mirror will become correspondingly transformed. It is obvious that if the man thought that the fault lay in the mirror or in the reflection itself, no improvement could take place. The unpleasant reflection would still be seen. Also, if he broke the mirror, he would still see the same unpleasant reflection in other mirrors: it would persist until he learned his lesson and himself became changed.

It is precisely the same with life. The outward life, circumstances and experiences are a reflection of the character of the individual, and until she alters her character the unpleasant experiences will persist.

Many people perpetuate their troubles by refusing to learn life's lessons, or, in other words to build up their character. They cannot see that the fault is in themselves. They cannot see that their character is reflected in all their work, and in all their dealings with their fellow men. What they put into life comes back, either in the form of harmony or in trouble and discord, according to the kind of character expressed. By altering our character, we become changed. Through being changed our work and dealings with our fellow men become correspondingly altered, and this, in turn, transforms our life. In order, then, to change the conditions of our life and thus replace disharmony with harmony, it is necessary for us to build up our character.

It must not be thought by any reader, because things are not going well with them, that they have done something wrong or wicked. All that it means is that their character needs rounding off and strengthening. The difficulties and troubles which beset them are splendid opportunities for the strengthening of character. By the overcoming of difficulty, we learn to be strong and self-reliant. By keeping our mind one-pointed on the goal of our ambition, not allowing either pleasure or trouble to distract our attention, we learn the value of purpose - we become purposeful, and therefore one of those who succeed and achieve.

When confronted by difficulty remember that, in overcoming it, you are becoming strengthened in character. Look upon difficulty as a splendid opportunity for development. The athlete develops his or her body and strength, by hard work. As they become stronger, they increase the weight of their barbells and the strength of their exercises. Look upon life's difficulties in the same light, and you will find no difficulty that cannot be overcome, and in the overcoming of which you do not become a stronger and better character.

Again, when faced by disaster, not only stand firm, believing that you are sustained by all the power of the Infinite, but examine yourself trying to discover what lesson it is that you have to learn. On no account pity yourself. Do not blame fate: do not look upon the disaster as evil, for it is only your highest good. Stand firm; learn the lesson which the painful experience has to teach, and you will never have to pass through the same trouble again. When once the character has been built up and strengthened to such an extent that you do not care whether the trouble comes again or not, you are free. "Unto him that hath (who develops and strengthens his character) shall be given, and he shall have more abundance: but whosoever hath not (who will not develop and strengthen his character) from him shall be taken away even that he hath (his character will weaken and depreciate)".

Chapter Twelve

The Value of Optimism and Cheerfulness

Pessimism and gloom are greatly loved by some people, yet, if they only knew how dearly they had to pay for these luxuries, they would not be so fond of them. One who looks on the dark side of things, and is gloomy, chilling in his manner, and low-spirited, little dreams to what extent this attitude of mind colours all his actions, or how it generates an atmosphere which drives people and opportunities away. Pessimism is destructive. If indulged in, it will, in course of time, reduce a man of ability to the very gutter of poverty and misery. Gloom and low spirits will effectually keep away opportunity, helpful people and friends.

The people who accomplish things and who overcome the apparently impossible, are always incurable optimists. Nothing can make them leave off trying, and nothing can either damp their enthusiasm or destroy their cheerfulness. Just as it is that those who are pessimistic and gloomy do not know how costly their failing is, so also the cheerful optimist seldom realises what valuable assets his optimism and cheerfulness are. Yet they are of enormous value to all who have to make their way in life. Optimism and cheerfulness are just as necessary for success as are strength of character, firmness, and a steadfast purpose. Without these valuable aids life cannot fail to be a tremendous struggle, for unless his abilities are of such an exceptional and high order that they compel attention, the atmosphere of the pessimistic person will effectually keep success away.

Success in any calling demands great application, dogged perseverance and tireless persistence. It is the incurable optimist who alone is capable of keeping on when everyone else is tired and gives up hope. The pessimist is the first to give up. "What is the good of keeping on", he says, "The thing is bound to be a failure". But the optimist refuses to be beaten, and keeps on, even in the face of every possible discouragement, and brings off the apparently impossible. Of course, even an optimist must mix sound judgement, good common sense and foresight with his optimism, for foolish optimism accomplishes nothing, except to provide material for the "comic" press.

Pessimism will bring even able people to the very gutter in want and misery. This is not an empty statement. Recently I came in touch with a most able man. He was educated, a fine writer, with wonderful and telling powers of expressions. He was also learned and could quote scientific authorities as well as the classics. I recognised that he was my superior in learning, knowledge, ability and culture. Obviously, he had the ability and education to occupy almost any position - but he was a pessimist. He had been a pessimist and a materialist all his life, and was apparently proud of the fact, yet what had his pessimism done for him? Was he, with all his fine gifts, education and natural ability a success? Was he prosperous, respected, honoured? No, he was, when I knew him, earning, as a labourer, a few shillings per week, not per day, and sometimes a little food. At night he slept on a concrete floor in a shed. He was so proud of his pessimism I had to ask him what good it had done him. I pointed out that if pessimism is such a good thing it ought to show better results. Whereat he was very hurt and would have nothing more to do with me. He, and others like him, cannot see that their attitude of mind drives people away, causing them to shun them. If a businessman needs a manager for his business, or an assistant for his shop, does he engage a gloomy pessimist? The men who are invariably engaged for these positions are bright, cheerful people, who attract customers so that they go to the shop again. Employers will never dream of engaging pessimists because they know that if they do, their business will suffer.

Pessimists, no matter how well-endowed they may be, soon find their proper level. They can never succeed in any undertaking that requires hope, vision, perseverance, sustained effort. They soon give up, declaring that the task is impossible. Is it any wonder that they fail in life, becoming, in course of time, mere flotsam and jetsam, drifting hither and thither on the sea of life?

It is, of course, true that some people are born optimists, and would be cheerful even if an earthquake had taken all that they possessed. No matter what happened they would still find something about which they could be glad, and would, instead of sitting down bemoaning their fate, immediately start repairing their shattered fortunes. It is equally true that there are others who are born with a pessimistic turn of mind, and experience great difficulty in being cheerful about anything. However, if we all had to remain just as we are born, life would be a sad business, but such is not the case. If we are born pessimists, we can change ourselves into optimists. If we belong naturally to the order of the lugubrious countenance, we can become one of the cheerful fraternity, if we will only take a certain amount of trouble. There are no difficulties that cannot be overcome, and although to change a born pessimist into an unconquerable optimist is, apparently, an impossible task, yet it can be done. It cannot be done in a week or a fortnight, but it can be accomplished in time.

All our troubles exist in our minds, and the troubles of a pessimist's life are due to his attitude of mind. If he can be made to see this, there is hope for him, but if he cannot, then his case is certainly hopeless. There is hope for the pessimist who realises that his attitude of mind has been driving people and opportunity away from him, at the same time sapping and undermining his own efforts. Having realised his weakness, he can set to work to change his mind. All his doleful thoughts must be changed into their cheerful and hopeful opposites. He must be forever raising his thoughts above the gloom in which he has hitherto lived, and thus take a brighter view of things. When he is tempted to say: "this thing can never succeed", or, "I can never do this", let him make definite statements to the contrary, such as: "this thing will and must succeed", or, "I can do this". Further, when everything looks black (as they do to all of us at times) let him examine the situation, looking for good points and redeeming features. If he will do this he will find much to encourage him, and for which he will be thankful.

Further, he must endeavour to see good points in other people. In the past he has seen nothing but evil or shortcomings in his neighbours, but henceforth he must endeavour to see their good points. If he will do this, he will be astonished at the number of good and noble souls that are around him, and how blind to their good points he has been in the past.

The whole process is most astonishingly simple, yet, if it is persevered with, it will, in course of time, completely revolutionise the mind and the life. As the pessimist changes into an optimist so will men and opportunity, love and happiness be attracted to him. Success will become a possibility, whereas formerly it was an utter impossibility. What is of even greater importance is that his value as a citizen will mightily improve. He will be able to render far better service to his fellows, either in his business or profession; he will also be a far more lovable creature at home.

This brings us back to the basic teaching of this book, which is that the outward life can be transformed only to the extent that we become changed within. Within each of us is the cause of all troubles, disharmonies and lack of success. First, we must become changed within, and become constructive, positive, harmonious, hopeful and cheerful thinkers. This transformation of mind, character and thought will entirely change our actions. In turn, the change in our actions will alter our life.

The way of success is first by constructive thought, followed by action and sustained effort, all directed by a strong purpose towards a definite goal. This goal must be an honest success, not through selfish striving, but as a reward for highest service to life and those with whom we share the eath .

Chapter Thirteen

Making Use of Infinite Power

There is an "inmost centre" in us through which we can contact the Infinite and harness ourselves to, what someone has called, the Powerhouse of the Universe. In order to tap the inner reservoir of power it is necessary to spend a short time night and morning and realising our oneness with the infinite and in calling upon it, thus becoming saturated with a spiritual energy that is greater than the life of man. This power is the inner essence of all power and therefore is intensely disruptive if used wrongly. It must, therefore, never be used for selfish aims, to dominate others, to attract wealth, or compel excess to come to us. It may, however, be used for the overcoming of our weaknesses of character and of our griefs and disappointments. It may also be used to increase our efficiency and worth and thus enable us to render more efficient service to life and our fellows.

It is useless, however, to rely entirely upon prayer or meditation or the Silence or whatever you may like to call this communing with the Infinite. First, we must draw power from the infinite, becoming filled and saturated with it, and then we must translate it into service. After becoming filled with power, we must express it in better work, greater efficiency, more faithful service. By so doing we express our real Higher Self, who forever communes with the Infinite. We bring it into every detail of our life. We express a new character in all our work, it reflects the perfection of the God within.

It is most important that one who learns the inner secret of Life and Power should be a practical worker in the everyday affairs of life. Avoid any form of mysticism that tempts you to withdraw from practical affairs, for this leads to inefficiency and lack of service, thus making the life a complete failure. You must express yourself in practical work and service.

Therefore, live the outward life to the full. Do everything in your power to increase your efficiency and therefore your ability to serve. Pay increasing attention to your work and to everything connected with it. Learn to observe what is going on around you. Take notice, arouse interest, in everything that claims your attention. Avoid daydreaming as you would the plague. Above all, be practical, always seeking for more efficient methods for producing better work and doing it more expeditiously. By so doing you will express the Divine within you and enrich the lives of others.

Part 2: Healing the Hard Times Consciousness

Hamblin Vision Publishing

Chapter Fourteen
Spiritual and Metaphysical Aspects

"Blessed is the man that
Walketh not in the counsel of the ungodly,
Nor standeth in the way of sinners,
Nor sitteth in the seat of the scornful.
"But his delight is in the law of the Lord;
And in his law doth he meditate day and night.
"And he shall be like a tree planted by the rivers of water,
That bringeth forth his fruit in his season;
His leaf also shall not wither;
And whatsoever he doeth shall prosper".

Psalm 1, vs 1-3.

Spiritual and Metaphysical Aspects

Mankind is suffering from a "Hard Times" Consciousness. The circumstances of many are deplorable, and there are comparatively few who are not affected. These "hard times" and this distressing state of affairs are not due to any failure on the part of God, or of nature, to supply the needs of the world's population. Actually, more wheat has been grown than can be sold. [1] Wheat has actually been burnt because it could not be sold, while at the same time thousands of people were starving. The bounty of God has not failed; it is the mismanagement of man that has brought about a farcical, yet tragic, state of affairs, in which plenty and cheapness abound on every hand, while at the same time lack of means debars so many from taking advantage of them.

All who live solely in the outer consciousness must naturally be bound by the laws governing material things, and subject to the calamities that afflict humankind. This should not be the case with those who are living the life of the Spirit. There is a way of escape, or, rather a way of mastery, for those who are spiritual children of God. This way is through realising the spiritual truth of the matter and living in the consciousness of this truth; with the enemies, fear and doubt, completely shut out.

---

1. This chapter was written in June, 1931.

Those who are in the mass-consciousness believe they are material creatures, living in a material world, governed by harsh material laws. If one is lucky, one is lucky; while if one is unlucky, one is unlucky; there is no possibility of altering it. On the other hand, the one who is spiritually awakened is, or should be, aware that he or she is a spiritual being, living in a spiritual universe, governed by spiritual laws. This person knows that they have a spiritual Father-Mother, who is the one source of all substance, and all wealth, who governs prosperity, who is the one and only real power, and who reigns supreme in the universe. They further know that the spiritual Father-Mother is love, is real substance, is divine order, and that such things as poverty, hard times and other forms of disorder are foreign to the divine idea and can form no part of their consciousness.

The cause of the trouble with many of us is that, in spite of the fact that we know better, we do not live in this higher consciousness, but allow ourselves to be drawn back into the material consciousness, in which state of bondage we are at the mercy of material conditions. When this is the case, it is impossible for God to help us, for we have departed from the pure spiritual consciousness in which God rules, and in which spiritual laws operate, unimpeded. It was, no doubt, because of this inability of God to bless those who do not live in harmony with His laws and who therefore are outside the spiritual consciousness, that so many appeals were made, in the Old Testament, to the Hebrew people "to return to the Lord".

> "Let the wicked forsake his way, and the unrighteous man his thoughts: and let him return unto the Lord, and he will have mercy upon him; and to our God, for he will abundantly pardon".
>
> Isaiah 55:7

God is always love, and mercy, and goodness, but He cannot bestow these upon us when we are outside of His presence and the pure spiritual consciousness. All the descriptions of curses and punishments in the Old Testament merely mean that by putting themselves outside God's love through wandering away through sin into the "wilderness consciousness", they became subject to all the disorders and disharmonies that are naturally everywhere present when God is put out of one's consciousness. The prophets used language which an undeveloped people could understand, and so they spoke of curses, punishments, and so on. Now we know that man punishes himself through wandering from the divine consciousness of good, into the "outer darkness consciousness", in which disorder of all kinds must be the rule, because it is an absence of the divine order. Therefore, we too have to "return to the Lord", or in other words, live in the Christ consciousness of good, of order, of love, and perfection.

We have to "return to the Lord" in our thoughts, for our thoughts must be prevented from wandering into weak or unworthy channels, and must be maintained in Heavenly places, if we are to remain in a Heavenly consciousness. But we have first to get our beliefs right, for if our beliefs are right, it becomes easier for us to hold, in our mind, the right thought because our thoughts correspond to our beliefs. Our thoughts being creative, it follows that our life corresponds to our beliefs, which being beliefs of Truth, produce conditions that are outward reflections, or "out-picturings", of the Divine order.

We have first to believe then that we are the spiritual offspring of an almighty spiritual Father-Mother; that we live in a spiritual universe, governed by spiritual laws, and that if we live in this realisation, we are set free from the carnal, material laws which govern in the outer or material consciousness. We have also to believe that the spiritual is the *real*. By "spiritual" I do not mean "astral", far from it, neither do I refer to anything connected with the place of departed spirits, but to the *real world*, which is the perfect expression of the divine idea, spoken of by Jesus as Heaven. "Our Father which art in Heaven", this is what we mean by the term "the spiritual is the real". Heaven is a reality, and all that is not like Heaven, is not of Heaven: it is a departure from it. We have to get this idea firmly into our consciousness that Heaven is the Reality, and that we are God's spiritual children, heirs of salvation, to whom the angels of Heaven minister. St. Paul said: "Are they (the angels) not all ministering spirits sent forth to minister for them who shall be heirs of salvation?" Edward Carpenter[2] caught a glimpse of this truth when he wrote the much-quoted words: "All the divine forces hasten to minister to our internal joy".

We believe, then, that we are citizens of Heaven, children, through a new spiritual birth, or awakening, of the God of Heaven, ministered to by the powers and forces of Heaven; and that because of this, we are set free from the law of sin and death, and the harsh material laws which govern those who worship Mammon.

There are those who are Christian and yet are enslaved by Mammon, because they believe in the power of money, and they believe that they are at the mercy of financial manipulations, depressions, and hard times. So long as they believe this and think in this way, they are led captive by the powers of materialism. Because a person is a Christian, it does not necessarily follow that they will be preserved from loss and calamity. They have to trust in God for all things, not only for the salvation of the soul, not only to be preserved from sin and self, and delivered from the enemies of the souls, and not only for bodily health, but also for all material needs, and for

---

2. Edward Carpenter was a hugely influential socialist, critic, writer, poet, thinker, vegetarian, and mystic. Not so well known today, he was a pioneering supporter of many progressive causes we now take for granted, including women's rights and sexual reform.

freedom from the effects of such things as world depressions and hard times.

In order to live in the higher consciousness that is in correspondence to that of Heaven we have to attain to it through experience and through constantly putting our trust in God. The first thing to do is to believe that such a thing is possible. If we do not actively and positively believe it to be possible, then it is obvious that it never can be possible in our case, for our mind is closed against it; and what the mind is closed against can never manifest. When, however, we believe that such a state of attainment is possible, then we open our mind to receive greater things: we push back its boundaries so that the apparently impossible becomes possible. At all times, we must remember that the invisible is the real, and, to the spiritually awakened, the outward is only an appearance. This is a reversal of worldly thought and belief. But spiritual truth can only be spiritually discerned. To those still unawakened, it is foolishness.

It is here that faith comes to our assistance. Faith is belief in the reality of the Invisible (the ever-present Heaven) and a hanging on to this one reality, in the face of exterior evidence that is entirely against it. Faith trusts in God, regarding all that is not like God and Heaven as an appearance only, which must pass away if truth is clung to and persisted in.

But the most important thing of all is to realise that we are living in a state of blessedness. We have to believe this and to keep on impressing it upon our mind and consciousness.

Without the blessing of the Lord (the Divine Good) nothing in our life can go right; but when the blessing of the Lord is with us, everything goes right, and even our mistakes are all overruled for good. When a state of blessedness exists then the disasters which afflict those in the mass or material consciousness cannot touch us.

In the seventeenth chapter of Jeremiah, we read that the man that departs from the Lord, and who trusts in his finite powers instead, is cursed. This means that he puts himself outside the blessing of the Good and True, the Real and Perfect; and because of this no real good can come to him. We are told that such a man shall be like the heath in the desert, inhabiting the salt and parched places of the earth. When the drought comes, he is helpless. He has no reserves of moisture upon which to draw, therefore the pitiless the sun burns him up and destroys him.

But, we read, the man who trusts in the Lord is blessed. That means, the one who trusts the *one invisible power of infinite good* instead of his own strength, cunning and wisdom, he is blessed. They are like a tree planted by the waters, that spreads out her roots by the river. When the drought comes it does not affect her; she does not even know when it comes, for her leaf is green, and she does not cease to yield her fruit. She does not have to be careful in the year of drought, for the reason that she is planted by the waters, and her roots reach to the river which never fails.

Here is a picture of the one who lives in a state of blessedness, who learns to live in the consciousness of divine good, so that outward happenings in the world of appearances cannot affect them. They are established in the inexhaustibleness of divine supply and bounty. Therefore:

> "He shall not see when heat cometh ... and shall not be careful in the year of drought".
>
> Jeremiah 17:8

One who can live constantly in the consciousness of Divine Good and Blessing is an adept. But adeptship is not as difficult as it sounds, and we can all arrive at this state, if we train ourselves, prayerfully, to abide in the spiritual consciousness of Truth. In any case, we can all turn to God declaring that there is only

> One Power, the Power of Good.
> One Law, the Law of Love.

These are continually operating. By declaring this truth, we do not alter either God, truth, or our real life. All that we do is to make it possible for us to enter into an understanding of Truth, and to realise the presence of God, which is divine good, ever present.

Chapter Fifteen

Psychological and Practical

This chapter is of a more elementary character. But it is necessary, for the reason that so many people are making life more difficult for themselves and others, through wrong thinking on the subject of hard times. Some know better, but still they do it. The majority are ignorant of the power of thought, and therefore sin in ignorance, so to speak.

In the last chapter I dealt with the spiritual and metaphysical aspects of the subject. This is at once the highest and deepest aspect. But the lower, shallower and more elementary aspect is also important, because it is a stepping stone to the higher. Indeed, it comes first, except in the case of established and consistent right thinkers, who know how to think, and practise it. These, naturally, always think rightly about every difficulty that arises, so that they become established in truth, and thus live in a higher consciousness that is unaffected, to a greater or less degree by material laws. But those who are not adept in the art of right thinking have first to learn how and what to think, before they can proceed to something higher and more advanced.

In this chapter I am not dealing with economics. We will leave them out of our consideration for the good reason that if people wait for a new system of economics, then they remain the catspaw of circumstances. Everyone, of course, should try to bring about a better system, for the sake of others, but we must not wait for any such change to help us, personally, to prosperity, because to do so would be to adopt a wrong and negative attitude, which would make our own recovery impossible. If a man expects to be helped, he can never succeed in life. The man who succeeds is one who never dreams of being helped, still less of asking others to help him. The only thing a man who expects to be helped is ever likely to receive is the old age pension - that is, if he lives long enough.

Another elementary truth that beginners have to learn is that one of the most prolific causes of failure in finance, health, and every other department in life, is self-pity. One who pities himself goes down and down, in every way. Self-pity is an acute negativeness that drives all good away, making its victim receptive to every form of negative ill, such as failure, loss, penury, loss of friends, etc.

Another negative evil is thinking that people are against us, and that life is against us, and that they are "doing us down". Such an attitude of mind also alienates its victim from all good. It makes him receptive to, and unguarded against, all kinds of negative states. This confirms him in his belief that people and life are against him, and they conspire to "down him" at every turn. A vicious circle is thus set up, from which he finds it impossible to escape.

It has been my privilege to meet several people who have become really and truly successful – soundly so – in life, and also numbers of life's failures. The successful people have all possessed the positive type of mind and mental outlook; while the failures have all, almost without exception, possessed the negative type of mind. The former went to the top because of their positiveness, the latter have all gravitated to the bottom because of their negativeness. Success, and with it prosperity, are the result of positive, robust thinking along constructive lines; while failure and penury are the result of negative thinking along destructive, hopeless, depressed lines. Success and abundance, on the one hand, and failure and lack, on the other hand, are manufactured in the mind by the thoughts we think, and by our mental attitude towards life and its experiences.

What people must learn is the basic truth that within themselves is the power to overcome every trouble as it arises: that they have within them something that is greater than their difficulties. They must learn that they can conquer and overcome in spite of economic laws, and world depressions. The text: "Greater is he that is in you, than he that is in the world", meets the case exactly. It sums up the whole truth in a few words.

Therefore, the first step in right thinking that we have to take is to refuse to think that we must be helped, or that we must wait for better conditions.

Men and women of business hinder their progress by thinking that they must wait for a trade recovery, or that they should be helped by the Government. They should instead affirm and realise that they possess a power that is greater than any limitation; or, rather, that there is within them the power that is supreme and which is the *only* power. "Locks, bars and bolts fly asunder", when this great truth is recognised and lived in.

People think and talk themselves and others into "hard times", and poverty and failure. The trouble is more psychological and mental than material. Their constant complaint is the "world depression". They recognise it as a dread master who enslaves them, and in whose grip they are powerless. Things never were so bad, they say, and they cannot see how they can possibly become better. By talking and thinking in this way about hard times, they weaken themselves, as well as other people, and make themselves receptive to negative conditions.

It is as though all humanity were being swept along on a great tide leading to loss, penury and disaster. Because they know not how to stem the tide of "adverse aspects" as some would term them, they are helpless victims of powers greater than themselves. They are swept along, and no one can help them, except by telling them the truth about themselves, and about God, *if they will listen*. But it is not wise to say anything if they are not ready for such information.

But all who will give heed may stop and stand still, while the tide of depression goes sweeping on. Let them say, quietly and dispassionately, but with calm conviction and faith: - "I affirm the presence and power of God".

When we recognise the divine presence and affirm the power of God, we take up an impregnable position. When we realise the truth of our position in God, we no longer want other people to help us, we no longer pity ourselves, we no longer complain that people are against us, or that life, or fate, is too strong for us. Neither do we want God to help us, in a weak sense, either direct or through other people. We believe that God "is able to do for us exceeding abundantly, above all that we ask or think, *according to the power that worketh in us*".

By the term "being helped, in a weak sense", I mean this. There is a positive way of being helped by God, and there is a negative way of appealing to God. The negative way is to pray to be helped and delivered, not through conquering and overcoming, but through having life made easier. This is destructive and leads to greater weakness and failure. The positive way is to affirm the thing as already accomplished in God, and then go forward in faith to achieve the apparently impossible through "the power that worketh in us".

Beginners may say: "I admit that I must think constructively, but how can I do it?" The most positive and constructive attitude of mind is that which maintains an attitude of faith. We need no great knowledge of psychology. If we turn to God, and then declare the truth about God, and about ourselves as children of God, we use our thoughts in a positive and constructive manner and establish our mind in the strongest possible attitude. And also, if we continue to think in truth and abide in truth, then we cease talking and thinking about failure, loss, poverty and "hard times". We cannot serve both

God and Mammon. If we are established in God, then there is no room for Mammon or any of his works.

Businessmen and women do themselves a lot of harm, and hinder their own progress, and also keep away prosperity that might otherwise flow towards them, by not only talking about hard times, but also by thinking and saying that there is no money about. I have met many negative-minded businessmen who never get on, and who always are wondering how they are going to meet the next quarter's rent. Their principal object, in conversation, has appeared to be to impress upon me the fact that things are in a bad way everywhere. They tell me that a certain traveller has said that things are terrible everywhere, or that they have heard that other businesspeople in the same town are doing very badly. And so, they go on, simply wallowing in thought and talk about failure, depression and hard times. They do it, I suppose, in order to excuse their own fall in business turnover. In effect, they say: "it is not my fault, it is due to general conditions of depression, and is quite beyond anyone's control". I have noticed that nearly all the men and womenwho are doing badly, and who seemed content to do badly, except to talk, are given to this destructive and negative habit of talking about bad trade.

But I have come upon a few who do not seem to be aware that there is such a thing as bad trade and a world depression. They are prospering; and the main reason why they are prospering is that they do not believe in hard times, or that *there is no money about*. This is a very important point because it is obvious that if a person of business believes that there is no money about, they find precious little of it. Through holding this idea, their thoughts revolve around it, and their actions conform to it, so that to them, in their experience, there is no money about, and things go from bad to worse.

But the other type of person does not allow this idea to dominate them. They believe that there is plenty of money about, and that what is needed is to get people to part with it. So, they act accordingly (with wisdom and prudence, of course) and prove that there is plenty of money and that it can be got through the use of vision, originality, energy, and service.

I have just received a visit from a professional man with a worldwide practise, as a consultant amongst big business firms. Ordinarily, he would be one of those most severely hit by the slump and world depression, because so many of the great companies are doing nothing, and therefore do not require the services of an expert. Yet, actually, his affairs promise to be more prosperous than ever, and last year was the best year he had ever experienced. I said to him: "This slump and world depression is almost entirely psychological, as far as the individual is concerned". He replied: "I know it. It is because I refuse to acknowledge the depression, that I am prospering, and making an advance, while others are making losses". This student has not only learned that life is mental and spiritual, and that what is held in the mind is manifested in the life, but *he also practises it.* He actually does what he has been taught as regards filling his mind with thoughts of success, progress, expansion, at the same time *feeling* that he is being carried along on a stream of good to ever increasing good. Because he is a doer of the teaching, instead of a hearer only, he is successful and prosperous. He reaps as he shows. So also does the man who allows the world depression and hard times to occupy his mind; only, in his case, the reaping is of a negative character.

I also know of a firm , who, when faced by a slump in business, refused to join in the chorus of lamentations that went up in their trade. Instead, they brought out a new article that was much needed and that was more efficient than anything that preceded it. In a week they were swamped with orders and booked up for months ahead. Also, by better organisation, they were able to reduce the prices of their other lines, so that they moved forward instead of backward. If they had allowed the virus of "hard times" wrong thinking to get its hold on them, they would have been as adversely affected as other firms. Yet, through right thinking, combined with wise and energetic action, and improved service, they went forward instead of backward - forward to greater achievement and an increasing prosperity.

But many of our readers may say that they are not in business on their own account, and that they are not professional people, but servants of a big company, and that therefore these remarks do not apply to them. They may point out that their particular industry is being "rationalised", and men and women discharged in consequence. How can this teaching help them? Again, there are thousands of others who are, apparently, quite dependent upon other people. How shall they act, especially if those upon whom they are dependent are of a negative type? Then there are the disabled, those badly injured in war, and those who have had very little education. How can they benefit?

In reply, let me say that the same law applies to all. If such people will keep their negative thoughts and ideas out of their mind, to be replaced constantly by thoughts and ideas of health, abundance, joy and achievement, then they will discover that mind is greater than matter, and that there is something within them that is greater than all their difficulties.

Others may have failed through lack of capital, through mistaken judgement, or through a series of misfortunes. Let such take heart. All things are possible to them. They can rise again, and will do so, if they do the right thing with their mind, casting out all fear, and all thoughts of failure, and establishing themselves in truth.

From this it is seen how important it is to hold the right idea in the mind, and to think and act accordingly. It makes all the difference between failure and success, and between poverty and abundance.

Now all this is very elementary, and is purely psychological, and not at all spiritual; but I have had to say it, because so many people do not think positively or constructively on the matter, and therefore act in such a manner as to increase their difficulties. I have said it, also, because this little book will go to many who lack even the most elementary knowledge about the cause of things. It will come as a surprise to such people to learn that they manufacture, to a very large extent, their own conditions in their mind.

But, having dealt with the subject in this elementary way, let us look at it from a higher standpoint.

> "The will of God expressed in man's body is life and health;
> in his mind it is wisdom, harmony, love, joy and peace;
> in his affairs it expresses as substance and success."
>
> - R. Linch.

The above is a good and fair statement of the metaphysical truth of the matter. God's idea towards us is infinitely perfect and good. God is not negatively minded; if he were, what a hopeless sort of universe this would be! God creates everything perfect. He is divine order itself; and, therefore, can express only divine order. There are no negative ills created by God. They are created on man's side. We need a cleansing of consciousness so that we should see and think in accord with the divine order. God creates health and abundance. Man, through his wrong attitude and thought, or through his material consciousness, turns them into their negative opposites.

The best way to keep out the virus of hard times and world depression is to fill the mind with truth. Remembering always that God is infinite and omnipotent and that God's will towards us is "substance" and success, our thoughts revolve around this truth, to the exclusion of the suggestions and mass hypnotism of the Hard Times mentality.

The student of Truth, that is the conscious child of God, possesses a great advantage over one who has to depend entirely upon psychology, because he can declare in the face of pending trouble and disaster: "Because I am a child of God, I refuse to entertain these suggestions of evil. I deny them a place in my mind, because they have no rightful place there. Because I am a child of God, I can never meet with any evil (I will fear no evil for *Thou* art with me, and where *Thou* art there is no evil) but all my ways are ordered by the Lord, I am upheld by heavenly (divine order) powers, and abundantly supplied with everything that I need".

God is the eternal substance. Wealth, supply, etc. are but a reflection of this reality in time and space. By turning to God and affirming the truth about him and about ourselves as children of God we gain the substance; after which the shadow can take care of itself. When we get our mind clear of error, and filled with truth, then everything else becomes automatically and harmoniously adjusted. We have to find the Kingdom of substance (God) first, then the other things are added.

To most readers this article must seem like a disquisition on psychology for worldly-minded people. But it is not so. All the time I realise that God is able to raise up and to cast down, to make rich and to make poor; but he operates through divine law, with which it is our privilege to work. We have to remember and to acknowledge at all times that the blessing of God is needed; and that without the divine blessing no good can come to us.

CHAPTER SIXTEEN

The One Power of Infinite Good

In order for healing to manifest in our life, and the state of wholeness to encompass and permeate it through and through, we have to turn to a power greater than ourselves. We have also to believe that this power is the only power. If we cannot at present believe it, we can declare it to be so. If we do this, then the truth of the matter is revealed to us later, generally in the midst of some trying experience. The reason this is necessary is a paradox. If we do not believe and declare that there is only one power, the power of infinite good, then we become conscious of other powers. By declaring the truth about God as the only power, the other seeming powers, or powers of a lower plane, are dispersed or destroyed.

In the Christ or God Consciousness of pure spiritual knowing of truth there are no such powers, but only the one power of love and good. By declaring the truth in spite of all temptations to believe otherwise, we enter the consciousness in which we know there is only the good. This paradox is a great mystery to all who cannot enter into the truth by means of spiritual knowing; but those who seek for understanding, acknowledging that spiritual things can only be spiritually discerned, will surely enter into a state of understanding. "In the world", said our Lord, "ye shall have tribulation: but be of good cheer, I have overcome the world". This might be metaphysically interpreted as:

> In the material consciousness there is trouble, disorder, want, failure and every form of disharmony to which you are subject to, or enslaved, to the extent that you remain or live in the material consciousness. But be hopeful with a sure and certain hope, for I have overcome the material consciousness with all its claims and suggestions of evil, disorder, and want, and have reached the pure spiritual consciousness of my Father, in which all is perfect, beautiful, harmonious, and Heavenly.

Because of this "overcoming of the world" we are set free from the power of material laws and enslavements to the extent that we acknowledge, believe, and accept the deliverance of Christ in the matter. Our salvation is a complete one, emancipating us from sin, from sickness, and from the power of Mammon, but only if we believe it and accept it, and enter into the consciousness of it. Until we do so, our creative imagination continues to bring evil, disorder and disharmony into manifestation: it brings us under the power of those influences from which Christ came to deliver us. When, however, we enter the Christ Consciousness which has overcome the world, or outer or material consciousness, our creative imagination is brought into correspondence with the Divine imagination which can only create that which is beautiful, harmonious, lovely and good.

Thus, we see that order and harmony, bounty and sufficiency, are brought into our life, not by our own mental power, but through the life, power, imagination and mind of God being allowed to manifest in a divinely normal manner. The divine word goes forth unimpeded and undistorted by man's contrary will and false imagination, to bring forth beauty, loveliness, order and harmonious perfection. "So shall my word be that goeth forth out of my mouth: it shall not return unto me void, but it shall accomplish that which I please, and it shall prosper in the thing whereto I sent it". And the result of this is a state of blessing poetically described by Isaiah: "Ye shall go out with joy and be led forth with peace: the mountains and the hills shall break forth before you into singing, and all the trees of the field shall clap their hands.

"Instead of the thorn shall come up the fir tree, and instead of the briar shall come up the myrtle tree: and it shall be to the Lord for a name, for an everlasting sign that shall not be cut off".

This describes a perfect state of blessedness, a complete healing of the whole life, through a divine adjustment, so that a state of harmony, wholeness and order is brought into being.

"Be not deceived", said St. Paul, "whatsoever a man soweth (in his inward thought and imagination) that shall he also reap.

For he that soweth to the flesh (the outward man and life that is not in harmony with God) shall of the flesh reap corruption (everything that is not of God comes to naught): but he that soweth to the Spirit (the Source of all harmony, order, beauty, and perfection, and Heavenly conditions) shall of the Spirit reap life everlasting (the life of God which is perfect order and harmony, and which can never grow weak or fade away)".

But how, it may be asked, are we to deal with life in the light of Scriptural teaching which is so at variance with generally accepted worldly wisdom? When faced by hard times and periods of financial difficulty, our first tendency is to shut up our pockets. We feel that we must not only cut out unnecessary and frivolous expenditure on ourselves (which of course is a right thing to do) but that we must also cease our liberal giving to the Lord's work. This policy is dictated by fear and doubt in God's goodness, and His ability to deliver us. If we adopt it, we encourage our fears, we increase our doubt in God (a deadly sin this), and thus make it impossible for good to flow to us. But if we continue giving, we keep the channel clear so that God's free supply can flow into our life. If we cease to give, we block the channel so that no good can flow in. I remember once receiving two letters by the same post. One was from a man in rather straightened circumstances, who wrote to say that he could not continue to subscribe to our magazine, the cost of which, by the way, works out at approximately one penny per week. I have never heard from, or of, the man since. How poverty-stricken his mind was in thinking that he could not afford one penny per week for a magazine which would have revealed to him, month by month, the knowledge that he needed to overcome his limited condition.[1] Such knowledge is acquired through regular reading and reflection. The truth is presented, month by month, in various forms and ways, so that in course of time the reader is able to understand and live it. Such information is not dearly acquired at the cost of one penny per week, and to spend such a sum would not be a great venture of faith. Yet this man, who had experienced a temporary setback, thought, in his panic and fear, that he could not afford this trifling sum.

The other letter was from a man who had lost all, and who was destitute, save for a few shillings. He sent almost his last coin in renewing his magazine subscription, declaring that he had decided to do so, as an act of faith. He almost immediately became the recipient of an unexpected £100. Cynics will say that he would have received the £100 in any case, but those who are experienced in the spiritual life, and in living by faith, do not believe that such would have been the case. Infinite mind knows the end from the beginning and does not see events one after another, one at a time, singly, as we do. Actually, there is no time or space, as we know them; therefore, God is not bound or limited by time.

---

1. *The Science of Thought Review*, circulated internationally by subscription, taught the fundamental importance of "right thinking" and how to transmute negative thought.

I give these two illustrations from memory; my description may not be exactly correct in every minute detail, but actually it is true in substance. Several times have I been astonished by people giving up their subscriptions because of temporary shortage of money. In their panic, they thought that they could not afford a subscription that has purposely been made so low that it amounts to about one penny per week. By so doing, and by so acting, they limited themselves in actual fact, and entered into a bondage of financial limitation.

On the other hand, far more often have I been amazed at the faith shown by many, who in the face of alarming circumstances have not only continued their subscriptions but have continued to help the work that has helped them; supporting it with a thankful heart, in order that its helpfulness might be extended to other lives. Such men and women of faith keep the channel open for divine good to flow into their life and affairs. They perform acts of faith, and, through so doing, prove God, who, when proved, is found always to be a God who never fails those who put their trust in him. Such men and women through their faith and acts and steadfastness of mind enter into a state of blessedness. Those who act differently, shutting up their pockets against the Lord's work (it does not matter which branch of the Lord's work is supported, so long as we give to it in a willing spirit) enter, not into a state of blessedness, but the reverse of this. In the Old Testament it is called a curse. I interpret this to mean that man, by his wrong attitude of mind and lack of faith, removes himself from the sphere of divine blessing, so that his life becomes like a barren wilderness.

The following is what God's word says concerning the blessing that follows tithing.

> "Bring ye all the tithes into the storehouse, that there may be meat in mine house, and prove me now herewith, saith the Lord of hosts, if I will not open you the windows of heaven, and pour you out a blessing, that there shall not be room enough to receive it".
>
> Malachi 3: 10

This is sufficient justification, I think, of all that has been written in this chapter. From this passage we see that by tithing we prove God, and He promises that if we so prove Him, He will bless us abundantly.

In concluding this chapter, let me say that I am dealing mostly with the inward and spiritual aspect of the subject. Outwardly we have to be "not slothful in business, fervent in spirit, serving the Lord". That is, we have to be industrious, do everything as unto the Lord, and do all in our power to improve our service, so as to deserve success and prosperity. But such industry as we display must not occupy all our time, otherwise we defeat the very object we have in view. Every day, if possible twice a day, we should sit quietly, realising the truth about God as our Father, and the truth about ourselves as children of God.

This may seem selfish to some readers; and to such it must be pointed out that we can best serve the world by being successful and happy ourselves. If we are weak, miserable, low spirited and in a state of failure and poverty, we are not in a fit state to help others. When, however, we have overcome, the very fact that we have passed through difficult times ourselves makes us capable of sympathising with, and helping and encouraging, those who are also passing through hard times and trying experiences.

The real source of supply is spiritual. Those who realise and acknowledge this know that the plenty that comes to them does not impoverish others, for the reason that the divine supply is infinite and inexhaustible. The divine abundance exhibited by Jesus in feeding the five thousand did not impoverish other people.

It can never be exhausted any more than the source of electricity can be exhausted, or the energy of the atom can become rundown and weakened. The divine power that heals can never be exhausted, and when a person is healed, he or she does not deprive someone else of his share of health. Those who can realise this, and live in the consciousness of it, enter into liberty.

Chapter Seventeen

Laying Up Treasure

Lay not up for yourselves treasures upon earth, where moth and rust doth corrupt, and where thieves breakthrough and steal: but lay up for yourselves treasures in Heaven, where neither moth nor rust doth corrupt, and where thieves do not breakthrough nor steal. For where your treasure is, there will your heart be also.

Matthew 6: 19-21

This passage has often been explained as meaning poverty and renunciation in this life, in order to reap the reward of eternal happiness in the next life. But such is not the true meaning. An understanding and realisation of its true meaning, not only saves the soul by establishing it in the eternal, but it also establishes our everyday life in a state of true and enduring supply of substance. This is so, because we become rooted in reality: we find the true and only substance, of which material supply and abundance are but reflections on the screen of time.

Our Lord tells us not to lay up for ourselves treasures on earth. This does not mean that we are to possess nothing, in a material sense. We may, or may not, possess anything of this world's goods, and we may be equally free, if our affections are set, and our attention concentrated upon, the reality that is behind all phenomena and this changing life, and not upon the possession that may or may not be ours.

There are two reasons why we should seek and find the true substance, of which outward supply and things are but a reflection, and they are these: -

Firstly, if we put our trust in material riches, then, because of the changeable and precarious nature of this present life, our whole thought-life becomes centred upon material things, so that the spiritual life languishes, and our real life (the life of the soul) dies; and then we are dead indeed.

We have all known men who were very happy when they were young and poor joyous Christians, always full of the joy of the spirit, and they showed it in their face and bearing. But then they became remarkably successful in their material affairs; and now the "cares of this life, and the deceitfulness of riches" have choked the word, and they are spiritually as dead as the dodo. Rather pathetically, they show us their property and their motor cars, talking to us about everything save the life of the Spirit. They cannot speak about this because they have none: it is dead, killed not by prosperity, but through setting their heart and mind upon it, thus neglecting the only Real and True. "For where your treasure is, there will your heart be also".

Concentrating and depending upon material wealth and possessions spell death to the soul and take away all real joy of life; for Mammon is a hard taskmaster. One who allows himself to become immersed in the cares of this world, no matter whether he be rich or poor, successful or unsuccessful, shuts out that heavenly vision; and not only loses all joy, but becomes as dead as the dead things upon which he concentrates.

If, however, we "lay up treasures in Heaven", that is, if we find God, the only true substance, instead of concentrating upon the fleeting treasures of the material world, we enter into a state of joy such as can only be experienced, for it can never be described. Our spiritual life also grows and flourishes, so that we renew our strength, we mount up with wings as eagles; we are able to run, and not be weary; and walk and not faint. But as for those who do not make this contact with reality:

> "Even the youths (the strong and well-endowed) shall faint and be weary, and the young men shall utterly fall".
>
> Isaiah 40:30

There is every reason then why we should seek God, reality, the only true substance. It is so obvious, and of such tremendous importance, overshadowing everything else, that the wonder is that the vast majority of people refuse to take heed, but to go on seeking satisfaction in the baubles of life, which never satisfy, and which only too often elude them, or break in their hands, so that they do not even have the opportunity of enjoying the fleeting delights for which they sacrifice all that is truly worth having.

There is another aspect of this subject, and this is its relation to health. The cares of this life are disruptive to health. Concentrating upon the things of this life, too much, to the exclusion of divine and causal things connected with our true life in God, destroys vitality and undermines health. This is why no weakling can win in the terrific struggle for material riches. Millionaires have to be tremendously strong or wiry, physically. Those who strive for wealth in the ordinary way have so many cares and anxieties, and the strain is so terrific, that their health, only too often, is undermined, so that even if success is achieved, they find that they have paid too high a price for it.

But this applies to all classes, to the rich and the poor, to the successful and unsuccessful, to the employer and the employee. All who turn their attention to material things, and do not seek the reality and the true substance, are cut off from their true life. Worry, care, anxiety, strain, all these destroy the health, and bring about breakdowns, if not serious diseases. "But they that wait upon the Lord" (the true life and author of life,) "shall renew their strength: they shall mount up with wings as eagles: they shall run and not be weary; they shall walk and not faint".

The second reason why we should lay up treasures in Heaven, i.e. seek and rely upon God, the eternal reality and substance, instead of seeking for, and relying upon, material wealth and worldly possessions, is this: when we seek reality, we find the *one source* of all supply and abundance. God is the supreme and only substance, eternal and unchanging. God-substance can never change, or fail, or pass away. Substance, the reality behind all supply, is the cause of phenomena. It is to supply, what the cinema film is to the screen. The pictures on the screen pass away. If the light fails, no pictures are seen on the screen, or if the focus of the bioscope is altered nothing can be seen clearly, but the film still remains, and can be reproduced at will, at any time. If we look upon the screen as life, then no matter how closely we may examine it, we can never understand it, for it is not real, but only a receiver of pictures which are reflected or projected thereon. If we would understand the mystery of the pictures which we see, we must look not on the screen, but into the projector. There we find the film which is the cause of all the phenomena. In the same way if we look at life as it appears, we can never understand it, and we find its phenomena ever changing and disappearing. We see something that we like, but if we try to grasp it, we find that there is nothing to grasp, and that already the picture has changed.

Therefore, we have to seek the reality, God, in order to find that which is real, unchanging and everlasting. When we have found God, we have found that which causes the phenomena, the reality behind unreality, the substance that is behind the fleeting things of life; that which abides the while other things fade away.

No observer of life can fail to have noticed how fleeting and unreliable are such things as riches, fame, popularity, possessions, material supply. One day we may possess a good business - the next we may have none. One day we may be in a lucrative position - the next we may be seeking a job. One day we may receive fat dividends from investments – the next we may find that they have all passed away. There is nothing substantial, certain, or real, about the so-called good things of life. If we depend on them, then, only too often, they slip through our fingers like sand. Some such experience as this is sometimes necessary, in order to make us think of, and appreciate, that which is eternal and enduring, and which nothing can shake or move. When our life is shaken up, and earthly props are taken away, we begin a search for that which is real, secure, enduring, and which can never fail us. We start our quest for reality.

What we call "supply", the wherewithal by which to live, is an expression or manifestation of an idea. Its insecurity and fickle nature are due to the fact that it is an expression of humanity's idea, which is imperfect. Our body, with its liability to ill health and disease, represents what we have thought about ourselves. Our changing circumstances also represent what we have thought about supply. These are not perfect because of our imperfect ideas and thoughts. There is nothing perfect, or enduring, in anything that is created by the human mind. Within itself it contains the seeds of its own death and decay. But the creation of God, the real divine idea and thought, is enduring, eternal, and forever perfect. A perfect God cannot create imperfection, nor anything in which there is death and decay. Everything exists forever perfect in reality, but, by our wrong ideas and thoughts, we divorce ourselves from this perfection. As Paul says: "all have sinned and come short of the glory (all glorious perfection, or divine order) of God". What is needed then is that we become united with the real and perfect, so that our ideas correspond with the divine. For supply we need to become rooted in internal and unfailing substance, the permanent reality that forever stands behind what we term supply. There is much solid, sound, definite and vital teaching, to this effect in the Bible. In the first Psalm we read: "Blessed is the man who walketh not in the council of the ungodly (those who do not trust God for everything); nor standeth in the way of sinners (those who fall short of God's glory and perfection): nor sitteth in the seat of the scornful (those who scoff at trusting in an available God): but his delight is in the law of the Lord, and in His law doth he meditate (bringing his thoughts and ideas into harmony and correspondence with divine truth, law and order); *he shall be like a tree planted by the rivers of water*, that bringeth forth his fruit in his season; his leaf also shall not wither; *and whatsoever he doeth shall prosper.*" The roots of the tree reach to the river, show that in a "hot and weary land", when the inevitable drought comes, it is unaffected, for it draws its nourishment from inexhaustible sources. By this allegory we are taught that it is possible to be rooted in the eternal substance, so that the droughts which come to the soul, and also to the outward man in the form of "hard times", and World Depressions cannot affect him.

"And whatsoever he doeth shall prosper", both in his spiritual life and in his outward life.

One who waits upon the Lord, and meditates daily upon His word, especially those parts that are strong affirmations of truth (God's precious promises), becomes strong and mighty in soul and spirit. He becomes conscious of a new power that thrills him, of an expansion of consciousness in which he knows that all is well. Also, he prospers in the outward life.

George Muller waited upon God, for the nourishment of his own soul, and was greatly prospered both in his spiritual life, in health of body, and as regards supply. Apart from nearly a million and a half pounds sterling ($7,500,000) or so, given him for his work, for which no appeals were made, his income rose from about £50 per annum to over £3,000 per annum. (Most of his income was given away). He had to pass through times of universal depression, but always he was maintained, blessed and prospered. [1]

George Muller did all this in order to prove to Christian people that God was still an available God. Each one of us can do the same. God is greater than any depression, greater than the intense difficulties that beset modern men in business, both employer and employed, and chief and routine workers. Their

---

1. **George Müller** (born **Johann Georg Ferdinand Müller,** 27 September 1805 – 10 March 1898) a Christian evangelist, was one of the founders of the Plymouth Brethren movement.

paths are beset with very great difficulties and uncertainties, but God is greater than them all.

Every difficulty must give way to truth, because truth is the only reality. Every time that we turn to God, we "lay up treasures in Heaven where moth and rust doth not corrupt, and where thieves do not breakthrough nor steal". If we take our stand in truth, refusing to give way, then truth by its own power demonstrates itself and vindicates our faith. But it is necessary to change the whole thought-life and consciousness, so that we think and live in the consciousness of the reality of divine substance. How can this be accomplished?

First of all, we have to give up certain habits of thought, replacing them by right habits of thought. The following is a list of the thoughts that have to be avoided. It must be remembered that thoughts represent desires, and these in turn arouse emotions. First there is the human desire, next comes the thought (which can be controlled) after which is aroused an emotion that cannot be controlled. By right thinking desires become transmuted, and emotions (if undesirable) prevented from arising. I shall therefore deal only with thoughts.

THOUGHTS TO AVOID

- Envy and Resentment
- Wishing (Day Dreaming)
- Self-pity
- Lust, Immorality and Passion

- Fear and Doubt
- Lack, Limitation

All the above effectively keep away prosperity and abundance. They eat out the very heart of a human being.

THOUGHTS TO CULTIVATE

- Good Will, Blessing and Benediction
- Achievement and Accomplishment
- Praise and Thanksgiving
- Consecration to God and Higher Service
- Trusting in God the Only Power
- Divine Inexhaustible Substance

The above help to change the attitude of the mind so that it becomes a magnet.

The above rough table gives some idea of what has to be done in the way of changing one's thoughts. In the course of time the new, constructive, positive, God-established thoughts filter into, and occupy the subconscious mind, so that a consciousness of truth is entered into.

It is necessary, at all times, to think of oneself as a spiritual being, inhabiting eternity, living in a spiritual universe, governed by spiritual laws. We cannot alter divine law to suit our own personal convenience, but we can work in harmony with it, so that only good, order, harmony and peaceful conditions manifest.

It is also necessary to state in words the truth about reality, about ourselves, and about life. Each one can say: -

> God is Spirit, and I am his child. Therefore, I am a spiritual being, inhabiting eternity. I live in a spiritual universe, which is governed by spiritual laws, with which it is my joy and privilege to work in harmony. Because I am a child of God, the only Substance and Reality, I am established in Eternal, Unchanging Substance, which always supports me in an Eternal Now.

Such a statement as this, gives us a consciousness of eternal being, in which we know that all is well, and that our treasure is in Heaven (unchanging reality); and that all our needs, both spiritual and temporal, are always abundantly supplied.

Then, as a result of this inward realisation - this living in a consciousness that the spiritual is the only real, and that spiritual law and Truth must of their own power demonstrate themselves, if relied upon - the outward manifestation follows. We may have to wait for it in patience, but:

> Rest in the Lord, and wait patiently for Him...
> Commit thy way unto the Lord, and trust also in

Him; and he shall bring it to pass...
Delight thyself also in the Lord; and He shall give thee the desires of thine heart".

Chapter Eighteen

Right Versus Wrong Methods

That it is possible for people to be successful and prosperous in life, who ordinarily would be amongst life's failures, has been proved, again and again. Those who would stand no chance at all when pitting their normal powers, abilities and wits against the best brains of their time, are able to succeed, be prosperous, and live harmonious lives, much to the surprise and wonder of their cleverer competitors. Actually, such people do not consider that they have competitors. They do not compete with other people, any more than the moon competes with the sun, or Jupiter with our own planet. The only things that they contend with are their own weaknesses; and even here they do not fight them but defeat them by building up their contrary virtues.

One who has a true idea of life has no competitors. He looks upon those who consider themselves to be his competitors as fellow servers of humanity. Because of this he wastes no time or energy in fighting competitors, but spends it on subjective work, which is one of the foundations of all true success and prosperity.

Even those who are not in business or in a profession may fall into the error of looking upon their circumstances and "shut in" environment as their enemies. They may make the mistake of fighting against them, and then are downcast because the more they fight their circumstances the worse they become. Fighting circumstances does but make them stronger. The only way to overcome them is to build up in the creative imagination a totally different state of affairs.

Many people make their circumstances worse by brooding over their troubles. This directs the life forces towards their troubles, thus building them up in greater power and might. Some make their troubles greater, and perpetuate them and intensify them, by praying about them in a wrong manner. They pray so much about their troubles that there is no room in their mind for anything else. Yet what is needed is a concept in the mind the very opposite of their troubles - a concept of that thing which they desire - a concept of victory instead of defeat, of achievement in place of failure, of harmony instead of disorder, of abundance instead of restricted means, of the inexhaustible nature of God's bounty in place of their ideas of lack and limitation.

George Muller, in his autobiography, said, during those times when his faith was tried, that they looked not on their apparent lack or poverty, but to the inexhaustibleness of a loving Father. Always, he acted in a positive way, looking to God, instead of at his difficulties; and, because of this, his mind was filled with concepts of God's abundance, so that he was always delivered, and that most mightily.

With regard to working subjectively, there is a right and a wrong method of prayer. One can hold one's personal or human mind up to the divine mind (nous), so that it becomes illumined and filled with divine ideas, which are always perfect. Thus, perfect ideas, none of which of course are anything like our earth-born thoughts of poverty, disaster and trouble, fill the mind, and these of course form the basis of the external life, bringing harmony and good into objectivity. On the other hand, the human mind can be compelled to make pictures of what the finite self thinks his perfection, and this can be willed into objectivity. But no good follows; for as soon as one trouble is apparently overcome, another one appears: and when evil has apparently been destroyed, it breaks out again, stronger than ever, but in another form.

The healing of the exterior life can take place only through a healing of the interior life. In other words, the human imagination must become conformed to the all-wise imagination: that is, the Christ or Divine Mind must be allowed to "do for us exceeding abundantly, above all that we ask or think, according to the power that worketh in us".

It may be asked, at this point, by some readers, how they can confirm their imagination to the all-wise imagination, and how can they avoid working with the human mind, against their highest good? The answer is that if we think of God and Christ, the eternal and perfect idea or word, and of a perfect heaven, in place of our difficulties, troubles and limitations, all the while acknowledging that God alone can give us a true concept, then it is given to us to know and understand truth, so that we receive a true concept of perfection. Every time that we turn to God in this way our ordinary or human mind is held up to the Mind of the Divine and becomes illumined. Thus, in course of time, we become heavenly minded; which, in turn, brings about a condition of heavenly harmony and order in the exterior life. First within, then without: first in the unseen, then in the seen: first in the Kingdom, then the "all things added". This is the divine way of change and regeneration.

Again, we can enter the more readily and easily into a consciousness of divine care and inexhaustibleness, through praise and thanksgiving. I know of nothing that so quickly opens the consciousness to an influx of the truth, as the act of praising God and thanking him both for past and present blessings, and blessings which are already ours in faith, but are not yet manifest. We all have innumerable blessings for which to praise God, but alas we have forgotten most of them. In doing so we have neglected God. We have been so busy trying to "get", that we have neglected to give. We have so wanted fresh blessings that we have forgotten to give thanks for those already received. We should make a daily practise of thanking God (our spiritual source) for all the blessings of our life from our earliest childhood onwards. Everything should be made the subject of praise and deep thanksgiving, even the experiences that have been most painful.

Particularly with regard to God's care and bounty we should give praise for the wonderful way we have been supplied all our days, in spite of our fears, and in spite of our faithlessness. Through thanking God for past mercies and bounties we gradually enter into a realisation that all our needs are abundantly supplied, both now and always; and that as children of the infinite and eternal we can never lack any good thing.

Then we can pass on to the prayer of faith, in which we thank God for the greater and more wonderful blessings that are already ours, but which are not yet manifest. In this we should take a large view, not holding any small ideas about God's bounty. If we go to the ocean of divine blessing with a teacup we obtain only a teacup-full of blessing, but if we go with a bucket, we receive a bucketful. When George Muller first began praying for his orphanage, he received shillings (25 cents); but before he had finished his life of continual prayer, he was receiving thousands of pounds sterling. As his ideas expanded and he looked for greater things, so did his supply increase proportionately.

If we expect great things from the Infinite and praise God for them, then they become possible of attainment. But if we neither claim, nor expect, nor give thanks for, great blessings, then they can never manifest, because we rule them out of our consciousness by our short-sighted and restricted outlook.

As we remember and realise what the Lord has done for us in the past, we cannot refrain from praising and thanking God for it all. We are also encouraged to enlarge our mind and ideas, so that greater things become possible. And so, we pass on from victory to victory, and from strength to strength, always in an upward direction, until we enter into full liberty and freedom.

When our life and circumstances are put upon a purely spiritual basis, we have nothing to fear, for actually and truly the infinite is our source. All our supply comes from our divine source, from spirit or mind, but it comes to us through mutual service, rendered in love.

I will conclude this chapter with a word or two upon "demonstration". People who keep on looking for results, who keep asking how they can make demonstrations, are like children who sow seeds in their garden one day and dig them up the next day in order to see if they're growing. Instead of looking for results, or thinking about results, they should keep on praying and seeking a realisation of truth, until they enter into a state of peace. What most people mean by "demonstration" is something definite in practical affairs achieved by declaration of truth, and through faith in God. But actually, the real demonstration is reached when we enter into a realisation of truth, when peace like a river flows into our soul, when joy unspeakable fills our heart, and we become conscious of immortality, and know that we're living in a timeless now, and that all is well, a thousand times well. At such times we know that we are upheld in the arms of divine love, even as the earth rests in the bosom of the soft atmospheres. A deeper breathing takes possession of our breathing, and a sense of power thrills us. All care and fear are laid aside, all the anxious framework of the exterior life is lost and forgotten. We just rest in the eternal.

This is the true demonstration. That is to say, when we reach this state of knowing, then the demonstration is made. Outwardly nothing may have happened or altered but the work is accomplished, and we can leave the rest with God.

If David had been able to abide in the consciousness of the 23rd Psalm he would never have had to write the 25th Psalm, in which he begs God to deliver him out of his troubles. If he had abided in the consciousness of ever present good that is breathed through the 23rd Psalm, his life would have been as calm and peaceful as Heaven itself. But he allowed himself to become agitated, hence his later distress.

We need to wait upon the Lord, to find the secret place of calm and true knowing, and then patiently await events, knowing that all is well.

CHAPTER NINETEEN

Laws Which Must Be Obeyed

He that trusteth in his riches shall fall: but the righteous shall flourish as a branch.

Proverbs 11:28

Living by the Spirit and upon the Spirit is not merely a matter of metaphysical understanding, but it also involves living one's life according to certain laws and principles. Life is governed by immutable laws. We cannot be blessed and established in Eternal Substance if we do not live in the correspondence with such laws.

The fundamental law of the Universe is love: not affection, but dispersive goodwill. By this I mean a giving of oneself to life and humanity.

When we accept this truth, our whole life becomes altered. A radical and revolutionary change of outlook takes place, for the reason that such an idea is entirely opposed to the ordinarily accepted standard of life's conduct. Only too often, the ordinary man wants to receive as much as possible, and to give as little as he can in return. No one who lives according to this principle, or, rather, lack of principle, can be either blessed, or established in eternal substance. If he is strong enough and sufficiently cunning, he may be materially successful, always at the expense of other people, but his life cannot be either blessed or peaceful. A continual warfare takes place, which increases in bitterness and intensity with the years. This is because the law of love and service is violated.

If our life is to be blessed, harmonious, and peaceful, we must live in obedience to the great fundamental law. This was perfectly expressed in the words attributed to Jesus: "It is more blessed to give than to receive". This means that giving or serving brings blessing to the one who gives and serves. This is because one who does so works in harmony and correspondence with the great law of life. If a person uses mathematics, according to the laws of mathematics, he obtains perfect results, but if he does not work according to the rules, then he obtains unsatisfactory and entirely wrong results. If a man designs and builds a machine or engine, according to the laws of mechanics, he obtains satisfactory results, and his machine or engine functions correctly. But if he tries to accomplish the same ends, and yet ignores the laws of mechanics, and works in opposition to them, this machine or engine will never work, even move a stroke.

Order and disharmony and also insecurity in some lives are due to working against the law of love and service. They keep on trying to benefit themselves, but all the while they are robbing themselves of peace and happiness and all of that makes life truly successful and worth living.

Actually, our principal concern in life should be to see that we give as much as possible. We should always give a fair price for the goods we buy and pay a fair price for the work that is done for us. Above all we should give in service as much as possible; such giving being done willingly and in love.

Those who are engaged in daily toil, or who work for a living, as it is called, should do as much as possible, and do it in a spirit of service to life and mankind. Those who have "means", can still serve in altruistic work. There is much that they can do, and in the doing of it they will obey the law of love, giving, and service. Everyone can do something or make something for others and thus discover, to their joy, the truth of the words already quoted: "it is more blessed to give than to receive".

Living according to the law of love demands of us that we exercise forgiveness, mercy, compassion, and that we never harbour such things as envy, resentment, or hardness of heart towards anyone in all the world. If we are to enter into reality, we must be love itself in word, and thought, and deed. This entails non-resistance towards those who would harm us. This is a difficult path, but it can be trodden by all, and it becomes easier the longer we tread it.

Having accepted the law of life, and brought our thought-life, our emotional-life, and our life of action into harmony with it, we are ready to advance into a realisation of truth, and to abide in reality.

It has taken me a long time to learn that actually life is not what it seems, and that it is in fact entirely different. Now I realise as never before that we must accept the Kingdom of Heaven even as a little child, without question, without sophistry, and without duplicity. Sooner or later we have to put our intellect and reason on one side and to acknowledge that spiritual things can only be spiritually discerned. This means that we have to exercise a different faculty by which it is possible to know, by direct knowing, things which the intellect could never accept. As soon as we start reasoning and arguing we get away from truth, and it becomes impossible for us either to understand it or accept it. It then seems absurd and impossible to us that life could ever be lived according to love and non-resistance, or that it is possible to live on the spirit and by the spirit. Yet, if we put our intellect on one side, and try to exercise our spiritual faculty of direct knowing, we receive flashes of understanding. These flashes give us glimpses of a life of wonderful freedom and spaciousness. We then realise that man does not live by bread alone, but by every word that proceedeth out of the mouth of God.

I am afraid it is not possible for me to explain any further. I speak of a great mystery. Sooner or later, you will come to it, for the veil of separation is getting very thin.

Chapter Twenty

Practical Instructions

In order to be able to remain stable in a world of transition and change we have to become established in that which changes not. It is only in this way that we can be upheld, and unaffected by outward disorder. We have to realise the truth about God and true substance, and the truth about the real man, who is a son and heir of God.

In what we call Heaven, or the *real world* which is the perfect expression of the divine idea, there is only perfect order, harmony, love, goodwill, cooperation, beauty and good. There is no such thing as poverty, finance, disease, ugliness or any form of disorder. This is because there is no sin there. That is to say there is no departure from the divine order or will. Everything takes place according to the will of God, which is perfect, for God is infinite love, wisdom, knowledge and power. God is infinitely whole and complete; therefore his true world of reality expresses his wholeness and completeness in the form of perfection and order, beauty and harmony, peace and joy.

Now the true man, that is, God's idea of man, or that which is truly man, and that which man truly is, inhabits this perfect realm and shares in its harmony and partakes of its bounty. God never created a poor creature, the victim of poverty or lack, and cannot think of him as such. God's idea of man is perfect, and it is through realising God's idea concerning him that man enters into liberty.

When we realise the truth concerning Man (the true man, God's idea), then we find that what is transcendentally true of Man is true in actual fact.

Man, the real man, the true idea of God, can never live anywhere but in his true environment. He lives in the only true Spiritual Universe, governed by spiritual laws, upheld and sustained by spiritual powers. As a child of God, all his needs are eternally and constantly supplied, therefore he can never lack any good thing. No evil can come nigh him, and nothing can hurt or destroy.

When we realise that we are really living in the true, spiritual world of perfection *now*, and that it is reality that is around us, and impinging upon us, we enter into a new life of liberty and understanding.

When man, through the exercise of his spiritual faculty of direct knowing, realises the truth of the whole matter, he becomes free. He is removed from the limitations of the sense-man; and then he knows that literally he lives by every word that proceedeth out of the mouth of God.

This is not mere talk, or a fantastic idea of my own. There are people today who are bringing Heaven into their lives, and who are living in harmony and peace, solely because they realise this great truth and live according to it.

Because it is true that we are spiritual beings living in a perfect spiritual universe, governed by spiritual laws, it follows that when we think, speak and act in correspondence with this truth we find that what we declare and hold to in faith comes into manifestation.

For instance, if we realise that man is always in his right place at the right time, we find that it is so, in our case, so that we never have to hurry, we always arrive at our destination at the right and convenient time, and that everything works together harmoniously, in a Heavenly manner. We may forget ourselves and still hurry at times, say, to catch a train, but if we do, we find that it has been quite unnecessary. The harmonious manner in which things and events work together seems uncanny or miraculous to one not used to the working of the spirit.

Again, if we realise that we need never be flurried, harassed or overworked, but always do our work at the right time, perfectly and without effort, we find that we are able to work without tenseness or strain, and that everything is accomplished well up to time, in a way impossible before.

Thirdly, if we realise at all times that a human being is a spiritual being, inhabiting eternity, a son of God, possessor of all the substance of God, we find that in our case it is an actual fact, and that our resources are the resources of God, no less.

We must get right away from the idea of money, or temporal riches. Money may lose its value at any time, and riches may flee away like the birds in autumn. We need to realise that we share the real, enduring, everlasting substance of God, our Father; that is, the real creative fountain of life, from which have sprung all the heavens and the worlds, and of which material things are but a shadow on the screen of time.

We should, on no account, think or worry about how, or in what way, supply is to come to us. We must simply meditate upon, and realise, the perfect substance, or the creative fountain, from which all that has ever been created, both seen and unseen, has sprung.

Some people waste a lot of time and energy in praying for say, £1,000 ($5,000). They very anxiously seek to "demonstrate" this amount. But, if they are successful, they may find that the money will not buy the happiness they had hoped it would. Indeed, it may seem that a curse has come with the money. We need to seek the substance, not the shadow: the reality of which money is but a shadowy reflection in time.

It is true that George Muller prayed for thousands of pounds sterling and received them; but I think if he lived today, he would realise that he needed something more stable and enduring than money, and that the only thing that could meet his need would be divine unchanging substance, and the real divine prosperity which is unaffected by human change.

But while it is not advisable to pray for money merely, yet we should "come boldly to the throne of grace, that we may... find help in time of need". That is to say, we should not be miserly in our attitude towards our infinite source of supply. We can take a teacup or a bucket to the ocean of divine supply. However much we receive can never make anyone else go short. We live in an age of plenty, even when life is regarded entirely from the outside, in a material way. Judged from this standpoint, one who has plenty, simply uses up some of the surplus material and goods which otherwise would have to be destroyed owing to nature's great productivity, on the one hand, and manufacturing overproduction on the other. Judged from a spiritual standpoint, there can of course be no scarcity at all. If we wanted material for a million worlds it would make no difference to Infinite Substance, which being infinite can never be reduced or lessened.

What we regard as material and solid, for instance, gold, or rock, or iron, is not so in reality, but is psychological and spiritual. So long as we think of material things as real and solid, they master us; but when we think behind them and regard the substance and reality from which these things spring, so to speak, we become free. The whole universe is really only "a something" in consciousness. The vast distances in space, which are so terrifying to some people, are nothing to those whose spiritual vision exceeds and encompasses them all.

But, going back to the matter of the £1,000, it may be argued that to pray for a certain sum is helpful and necessary in order to focus the mind and attention upon a definite point. This being necessary, because if prayer is diffused, then the mind is not concentrated, and no results follow; Whereas, if prayer is pointed and definite, the mind is concentrated and focused so that results do follow.

This criticism is a fair one. It is necessary to concentrate and focus the mind if results are to follow. It is, however, much better to focus the mind upon the substance rather than upon the symbol. Those who cannot concentrate upon the reality which they cannot see, or who cannot think in an abstract way, had better concentrate upon something that is definite and concrete to them, and tangible to their imagination and understanding. Someone may need a home, a really nice home. Let him, however, concentrate upon the home, and not upon the money that is necessary to acquire it. Let the divine spirit find both the place and the means. This mode of working with the invisible power of prayer, will do for a time. Later on, it will give place to something more advanced.

One thing is common to all methods of, as it were, "living upon the invisible", and that is that the idea of perfect abundance and security must be focused, formed, crystallised and then projected into the Invisible. Then it must be held there, and perseveringly so, in spite of discouragement, fears, and all sense evidence that proclaims loudly to the world that all our faith is in vain, and that we are merely chasing a will-o-the-wisp. He who boldly, yet humbly and reverently, holds the idea of divine supply, up to God, or holds it projected into the invisible, unwaveringly, at the same time realising that he is at the secret fount, the one source of creative life, from which all the heavens and all the worlds proceed, will surely see signs following.

A time must be set apart each day for quiet a meditation upon truth, until the sense of realisation comes and with it a feeling of joy, freedom and uplift.

This sense of realisation must also be recalled from time to time during the day by means of affirmations or short statements of truth. These maintain the soul in a state of faithful realisation and also keep out thoughts of doubt and fear.

I find that meditation upon the word of God is the most powerful help to realisation. The 1st Psalm, also the 23rd, the 37th and the 91st are all most helpful. A whole Psalm may be read at first, but after that I find it better to concentrate a upon one or two verses until the sense of realisation comes, and I feel as joyous and uplifted as though the greatest of demonstrations had just been made. The fact that outwardly our circumstances may be very difficult should not be allowed to reach us, or to upset the calm state of mind that our meditation has won for us. The real demonstration is the realisation that we enter into in our time of meditation and silence. First in the unseen, then in the seen. First we learn to live in a state of realisation of divine truth, and then, later on, truth manifests itself by its own power.

The idea upon which we meditate and hold in our minds is, of course, that God is infinite in power, resource, love, knowledge and wisdom, and is the one fountain of life from which all manifestation proceeds: that he is the eternal substance, of which all that is considered concrete, such as gold and other metals, food, materials for clothing, and so on, is but a reflection in time. We meditate upon this great truth of reality and true, unfailing, inexhaustible substance until we become consciously rooted in the eternal, and know ourselves to be children of eternity, instead of creatures of a day.

Then our short, sharp statements are such as to recall to our mind and consciousness the great truth into which we have entered in our times of meditation.

> "The Lord is my shepherd, I shall not want."

This is a helpful affirmation. If you choose you can alter its wording, such as the following:

> "The omnipotent love enfolds me and supplies all my need."

If the 91st Psalm is committed to memory, one or another of its verses will rise into consciousness just at the right time, to meet each situation as it arises. By persevering in this way, we gradually become able to live in a consciousness of divine good and inexhaustible supply, which we know must manifest always at the exactly right moment.

Just a word of warning here. There are some people who seem able to demonstrate results beyond their stage of spiritual growth and development. Such should be careful not to claim too much, for, if they do, their success may unbalance them. Such should go forward step by step; each one a small advance over present limitations. At all times it must be borne in mind by all who seek to use the spiritual power and forces of prayer, that the object to be aimed at is not to be wealthy or worldly powerful, but free from the tyranny of wealth and Mammon. Wealth, show, vulgar ostentation, large possessions are anathema to the true child of the Spirit. The simple life, lack of ostentation and adornment, the use of things that are plain, good, but not showy, sober conversation, all these are signs of spiritual progress, and real refinement. They are the outward appearances of the solid, real and true.

But this will hardly interest many readers, for the reason that their sole thought at the moment is to find some sort of anchorage amidst the troubled waters of the present time, or some firm place of security within the quicksands of life as it is today. The message to such is: become grounded in eternity. Acknowledge yourself to be a child of God, living in Eternity, supported by Divine forces and ministered to by Heavenly Powers. A child of Heaven can never lack any good thing. He has access to the Power that created the Heavens and worlds innumerable, for "all that I have is Thine". It is only when man thinks he is separated from his divine source, thus losing his heavenly vision, and allowing himself to think in terms of doubt and fear and in an "earthy" way, that he becomes a victim of the forces which govern this material world, enslaving mankind in a grievous bondage.

Remind your soul constantly that the 'real' you can never lack, any more than God can lack. Endeavour also to get behind the seeming and to realise that all material things are but a reflection of that which is psychological and spiritual, that the invisible is the real, and that what is meditated upon in the unseen, later becomes manifested in the seen.

Remember also that those who receive from the unseen must not withhold their giving. The channel must be kept clear at all times. Those who would be free from the clutches of Mammon must not hoard, clutch, grasp or practise acquisitiveness.

> "There is that scattereth, and yet increaseth; and there is that withholdeth more than is meet, but it tendeth to poverty."
>
> "The liberal soul shall be made fat: and he that waterereth shall be watered also himself".
>
> Proverbs 11: 24-25

Part 3: True and Lasting Success

From Simple Talks on Science of Thought No. 8

Hamblin Vision Publishing

CHAPTER TWENTY-ONE

True and Lasting Success

There is no failure in anything God does. Infinite wisdom is incapable of doing anything imperfectly. In the Spirit, or in the *true realm* of which we have already spoken, perfect order reigns supreme. Everything is in its place, doing its work perfectly, just at the right time, at the right moment, and doing it perfectly. The supreme mind can never make a mistake, be guilty of an error of judgement, or fail in any of its undertakings.

No failure possible

In the real world of the divine order there neither is, nor can be, any failure. All is success. It does not matter how, but in some way, we have fallen in consciousness from this ideal perfection in which we were created; consequently, we fail in many ways, and are unsuccessful to a certain extent in all our undertakings. It is necessary to understand that God never created imperfect sons and daughters. Each one of us has been thought into being by the one Father-Mother, (or God) as a perfect child in the world of ideation – which is the real world. This real world is not a place afar off but is here. It is really a state of consciousness.

In the perfect world of reality, we have our place as a son or daughter of God. If we are literally and actually sons and daughters of God, then, so long as we realise this truth, live in the consciousness of it, think in harmony with it, and keep in touch with this plane of perfect ideation, we can never actually fail, and our life must be in the truest sense of the word successful.

What success is

First of all, what do we mean by success? A successful life may be described as one in which the greatest amount of harmony is expressed. Many make the mistake of concentrating upon material success. This they may gain, but at too great a cost. Successful in one direction, they are unsuccessful in others. I have known many people, successful in material things, whose life in other respects has been a literal hell; of others who have, in their fight for riches and power, lost all capacity to enjoy the real things of life.

Success: true and false

It is a good thing, however, to have a healthy ambition in life, and to be successful in our calling or profession; but to concentrate wholly upon material success spells death to all the finer capacities of true enjoyment and happiness. In addition to bringing harmony into the life, true success must also bring lasting satisfaction. While it is not possible to define the word "success", yet each one of us has an idea in our hearts of what success means to us. If at the end of life, we are satisfied with what we have achieved, we may safely conclude that it has been a successful one.

All can be truly successful

It is not given to all of us to be either great, rich or famous. Most of us would rather not be either. But each in their own way may be successful.

How then can we make life yield up to us that contentment and happiness for which we have an inward craving, and which to us would be true success? How can we stop the horrible failure which seems to dog our footsteps through life? Mere hard work will not do it. Toiling early and late, seven days a week, will not accomplish success. I have known people who have done this for years, and then have lost every penny they possessed. Capacity for work and staying power are very necessary, but of themselves will not bring success.

Material success is not everything

Even if material success were won by such means, the life in other directions would be in ruins. If the whole of the attention is directed to material things, then other departments of life go wrong, or we lose all capacity for enjoyment; therefore, our life cannot be called successful, or yield to us any satisfaction.

Two thousand years ago there came one who taught the only way to a real, lasting and satisfying success. This teaching has been too advanced for the mass of people, for only a few have followed it. Possibly more are ready today. In any case, no other method can achieve the desired result. Much of the teaching of psychology and so-called spiritual science with which the world is deluged today can only result in increasing and multiplying the misery, strain and disorder of life on this planet.

It can produce no other result, for it endeavours to alter life according to human wisdom, by the use of interior mental and spiritual powers. The result can only be disaster and chaos. One person says to himself: "Before my life can be harmonised, I *must* have money". Another declares: "Before I can be happy, I *must* get me a husband". Yet another, "If I am to be happy, I *must* obtain a divorce". Still another: "I *must* get my son a good position". And so they sit in the silence, calling upon great powers and forces, in order to put the world and their affairs "right", according to their poor, human myopic sight. And what is the result?

Those who set out to get money find the fruits of their labours as bitter as gall. The one who *must* have a wife, and the one who *must* get rid of a husband, sit down at last amidst the ruins of their happiness in the depths of despair. All disillusioned, all desolated, with happiness farther off than ever – apparently gone for ever; although this is not so in reality, for it is possible to "forsake our ways" and get back into the right path. Christ's recipe for successful living was that we should first find the inner Kingdom, after which all things desirable will be added to us. This inner Kingdom is the world or realm of perfect order and ideation. The realm where both we and our life are forever perfect.

The secret of true success

The truth of Christ's teaching is at once apparent, for it is obvious that if we can only get in touch with this inner perfection, and bring our thoughts into harmony with it, then our life on this material plane must reflect the Divine Order. One who gets in touch with the inner harmony is guided by the Wisdom that is infinite. Consequently, no mistakes are made, and no disorder created. All will admit that failure in life is due to wrong decisions. After a ghastly failure, we say: "If only I had decided differently all would have been well". Our failure has been due to a wrong choice.

Wise decisions

So long as we are guided by finite wisdom this must ever be the case; for, not knowing all the facts of the case, we cannot of ourselves make a right decision. But if we make contact with the inner realm of perfect ideation - the Christ-realm of Perfection - shutting out all thoughts of exterior things, wisdom and ideas come to us from this Higher Plane through our super-conscious mind, and if we follow these all is well. Naturally this cannot be learnt in a day, but it can be mastered in time. Until such time comes, one can be helped considerably by working according to the following rules:-

1. Choose that course which is best for the community.

2. Choose that course which is conducive to our highest good.

3. Mix common sense with your decisions. Do not be too altruistic at first especially. But always keep your face to the light, and strive and aspire after the good, the beautiful and the true.

By following the above, you may experience temporary loss, but ultimately you will gain.

One who follows the good and true is helped by invisible forces; everything works together for good, and all that is evil in his life is transmuted into good.

Just think over the above remarkable statement. Although the teaching of Christ is so simple, yet it is not easy to follow, simply because it is opposed to worldly ideas. Worldly wisdom can never bring true success. The writer is acquainted with the private life of those whom the world looks upon as wonderfully successful, and they are full of trouble and dissatisfaction. Therefore, it is only the Christ-way that can bring real and lasting success and happiness. Although this way is difficult in one sense, it is the easy way after all. It accomplishes with ease that which men with tremendous strain and effort are attempting to achieve, but all in vain.

The easy way

It is the easy way, for, by uniting ourselves with the Infinite Power, we become channels for its expression. We do not have to slave and toil, becoming weary and worn out, but we simply allow the Infinite Power to work through us. All that we have to do is to be persistent in linking ourselves up to the powerhouse of the universe. Wisdom and power, ideas and guidance, are all ours if we will only make use of them. *The truly successful life is also the carefree life.*

Chapter Twenty-Two

Also by Henry Thomas Hamblin

The Stillness of the Infinite

The Message of a Flower

The Secrets of Your Divine Powers

Please visit www.thehamblinvision.org.uk to purchase the following titles:

ALSO BY HENRY THOMAS HAMBLIN

The Way of the Practical Mystic
The Little Book of Right Thinking
The Power of Thought
My Search for Truth
The Story of my Life
Within You is the Power
Life Without Strain
Divine Adjustment
The Open Door
Life of the Spirit
His Wisdom Guiding
The Hamblin Book of Daily Readings
God Our Centre and Source
God's Sustaining Grace

Thank you for purchasing this book. If you have enjoyed reading it, please consider leaving a review. It takes just a moment, and helps small publishers like us boost the visibility of our books, so that other readers can find our titles. Thank you – your time is much appreciated.

You can scan this QR code by holding your phone's camera to the code. A prompt will appear, which will take you directly to the 'leave a review' page.

To review in the UK please scan the QR code or follow this link

156 THE SPIRITUAL PATH TO TRUE SUCCESS

To review in the US, please scan the QR code below or follow this link.

www.ingramcontent.com/pod-product-compliance
Lightning Source LLC
Chambersburg PA
CBHW060607080526
44585CB00013B/714